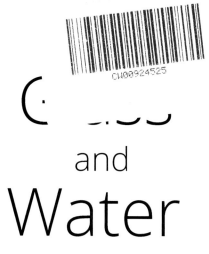

Glass
and
Water

The Essential Guide to Freediving
for Underwater Photography

Mark Harris

With a Foreword by Dan Bolt

Slip through and reach

[signature]

ISBN 978-1-909455-10-8 (Paperback)
ISBN 978-1-909455-11-5 (EPUB ebook)
ISBN 978-1-909455-12-2 (PDF ebook)

Cataloguing-In-Publication Data A catalogue record for this book can be obtained from the British Library.

Cover Design copyright Dived Up. Photos by Laura Storm.

Printed by Bookpress.eu, Olsztyn, Poland.

Published 2015 by

Dived Up Publications
Oxford • United Kingdom
Email info@divedup.com
Web www.DivedUp.com

Table of Contents

About the Author

Mark first learnt to freedive at the age of ten in the blue waters of the Bahamas. Growing up surrounded by warm, tropical oceans and a myriad of marine life, meant endless childhood days were spent snorkelling among the coral gardens. His developing fascination ultimately led to scuba diving and, as luck would have it, a youth apprenticeship working the summer season on a local dive boat. It was during those early years that Mark's ability as a freediver began to emerge.

After relocating back to the UK in the mid-seventies, he ventured briefly into the Royal Navy before pursuing an independent career in IT. Outside of his career, his interest in scuba diving continued to grow and, with that, a passion for underwater photography.

In 2002, Mark returned to his roots and began training to compete as a freediving athlete. Over a ten year period he became the UK champion four times, set a number of British freediving records and won a silver medal for the UK at the AIDA World Freediving Teams event in 2004. These successes led quite naturally to a variety of challenges. He ran London's longest standing freediving club between 2004

Mark Harris

and 2012 and has instructed, coached and judged at national and international competitions. He has also enjoyed teaching in the television and film industry, including Guy Pearce for his underwater breath-holding scenes in 'Houdini'.

During his time as a competitive freediver, he acted as Press Officer for the British Freediving Association where he liaised with the press, public, media, sports and medical bodies on a regular basis. His expertise has been sought on a host of wide-ranging topics from a David Blaine underwater stunt to the 2006 bombing tragedy in Dahab. He has written several related features and news articles.

He is a member of the British Society of Underwater Photographers. Mark is married to his dream girl, adventurer and underwater photographer Laura Storm. They live together in Surrey, UK.

Acknowledgements

I have had far too much help with the production of this book to now fail in expressing my gratitude. Ideas and concepts are fine at the outset of a project like this, but forming them into a finished product needs a bit more skill, effort and vision. In this case that has come from a team of unique people.

I can only start with the person whose name should have appeared on the cover as co-author, but who refused to let me do that — my partner, Laura Storm. As well as tirelessly reviewing every word, her images are present throughout the book. More than this though, the journey I have taken on this project is one she has accompanied me on at every step, through thick and thin.

Without my publisher Alex Gibson, *Glass and Water* would be a collection of files on my laptop, destined for tomorrow's list of things to do. I couldn't ask for a better working relationship than the one I have had with Alex.

There have been many contributions to the book, in the form of images, articles, introductions, reviews and illustrations. For these I would like to thank Doug Allan, Samphire Amps, Dan Bolt, Fred Buyle, Paul Colley, Martin Edge, Adrian Finnegan, Danny Kessler, Anne-Marie Kitchen-Wheeler, Pierre Lambreth, Terry Maas, Jan Nygaard, Brian Skerry, Andrew Sutton, Takuya Torii, Steve Warren, Shane Wasik, Jamie Watts, and Sheila Wisdom.

Although it isn't possible to thank individually all those who have encouraged, inspired or supported me in this venture, I'd still like to express my thanks to everyone who has.

Finally, there are three people I want to thank for their fundamental contribution to *Glass and Water*, and so much more. For providing me with the opportunities in life that bring me to this point I would like to thank my parents Patricia and Michael. I also include my younger brother, Martin. I made a promise to him to continue with the work he started in photography, before his passing away. For Mum, Dad, Martin and Laura, I dedicate this book with my love.

Foreword

Take a deep breath, relax, and we shall begin. Imagine yourself gliding effortlessly through sunlit turquoise waters, almost able to feel the light itself rippling over you as you approach your subject. Silently, carefully, gently, you get close enough to frame a few shots with your camera; capturing your quarry in a natural, intimate and respectful way. Perhaps there is even enough time to lower the camera and admire the moment you are sharing with the marine environment before heading back to the sun-lit world above you for that beautiful lungful of fresh, life affirming air.

Wow, sounds good doesn't it? Okay, so it is perhaps romanticising in some small way what can actually be achieved with proper training and discipline by a freediving photographer. But it is by no means beyond the realms of possibility for anyone wishing to pursue underwater photography, either as a hobby or a career, to reach this level of skill with the minimal amount of kit that freediving requires.

I discovered the serene, but energising sport of freediving at the same time as I discovered an interest in underwater photography. Having been a scuba diver for over a decade when I took my first freediving course in 1999 in the chilly waters off the coast of the UK, the benefits of leaving the cumbersome, heavy and noisy open-circuit kit back on the beach were immediately apparent.

It was just a few short years later, in 2003 and 2004, that I was helping to run international freediving competitions in the clear blue waters off Cyprus and watching the top-flight competitors setting world record after world record. Not being there to compete gave me the opportunity to freedive with, and photograph, some of the giants of freediving: Fred Buyle, Herbert Nitsch, Carlos Coste, and the late, great Loic Leferme to name a few. Sharing these experiences with true proponents of the sport and its roots, taught me that freediving gives the submerged 'aquatic ape' enhanced senses seemingly at odds with one-another. At the same time as revelling in a beautiful sense of serenity, the freediver also becomes acutely aware of their surroundings with heightened alertness of, and respect for, the marine environment and the many amazing creatures it is home to.

It was at these competitions that I first met Mark; he was there as part of a large British contingent and representing a growing enthusiasm and respect for the sport 'back home'. Over the few short, busy days of the event he witnessed the ups and downs of the competitive side of the sport, but this was just the start of his notable career in freediving and I know it was a truly memorable event for both of us.

It was also at this time that my enthusiasm for freediving for underwater photography was really taking off. Competent, disciplined and well-trained freedivers make for great photographic subjects, and Mark was no exception. Above all I was learning just how important the seemingly small nuances around kit selection, buoyancy, in-water attitude, breath-control and mental state all are for successful photography below the surface without the need for scuba kit.

In the intervening years Mark and myself have both been keen freedivers and underwater photographers, Mark majoring more on the freediving and myself more keen on the underwater photography. We have both enjoyed success as a reward for training and constant self-improvement; Mark has gone on to hold many British records and I have won the British Underwater Photographic Championships on two occasions, both times using nothing more than my mask, snorkel and fins (and camera, obviously!).

In my opinion there are few people better placed to write a book such as this than the author himself; drawing from many years as a well travelled, accomplished freediving underwater photographer has given Mark the insight into just what it takes to make this combination work.

Glass and Water gives the reader the tools to develop a healthy appreciation for the marine environment by using the three R's: 'Research, Regulations and Respect'. This basis of respect is a theme which runs through the book and is probably the most important factor upon which all accomplished freediving underwater photographers can base their success.

With chapters that cover the essentials of in-water safety, kit selection and correct usage, as well as detailed descriptions about the 'art' of freediving (by art I mean the ability to make every movement seem effortless, natural and purposeful but almost without conscious thought). Mark will most definitely help you to improve your efficacy as a freediver. Note however, I have not said 'will improve your breath-hold time' — as he also discusses the dangers of getting distracted or being tempted to stay for 'just one more shot'.

Equally, the areas of the book that delve into underwater photography will help both the seasoned underwater shooter to think more specifically about how to change their approach for breath-hold diving, as well as guide the novice snapper around some of the pitfalls of equipment selection and give a sound basis for shooting engaging images.

This title shouldn't be viewed as two separate instructional books that have been printed together. There are areas of discussion that take in what the two disciplines offer when used together; for example Mark takes a look at the challenges and opportunities for freedivers, as well as discussing how to approach various inhabitants of the sea in order to make the best of those magical moments where freediving and underwater photography really can lead to something special.

All the way through the book Mark takes the time to make what you are learning about freediving completely relevant to underwater photography. Every hint, tip and instruction in this book is there for a very good reason, and based on Mark's own proven successes.

Finally, don't just think the techniques you will learn about are only relevant for warm, blue waters. Being a UK based freediver Mark is no stranger to cold, gloomy waters (believe me we have plenty of opportunities to encounter them!) and this has a bearing on all the areas covered in this wonderful title.

Come on in, the water's lovely!

Dan Bolt
May 2015

Having been brought up on the south western coast of Britain, the sea has always had a huge influence on Dan's life. Learning to dive at thirteen years old was the first step on a life-long journey of discovery and unending fascination with the marine environment which has led to him becoming a multi-award winning underwater photographer, a regular contributor to diving magazines and co-author of *Nudibranchs of South West England* (2014, with Terry Griffiths and Bernard Picton).

Glass and Water

Introduction

Having been privileged to win awards in competitive freediving over the years, I have realised that much of the equipment and techniques lend themselves well for the benefit of the underwater photographer when not using scuba. I felt inspired to write this guide. I also realised that these benefits could be exploited at all levels, from the fledgling snorkeller to the heavily equipped specialist. Knowing that the popularity of underwater photography while freediving is increasing rapidly, and as an underwater photographer myself, it struck me that there were horizons to be expanded for all.

I have used the 'freediving' term quite liberally throughout, and I was initially hesitant to do this. Many people equate freediving with the competitive side of the activity, where young athletes with seemingly superhuman breath-holding abilities, challenge each other to reach depths well beyond those of recreational scuba divers. Entering this domain would be difficult for many to envisage; feeling restricted by age, breath-hold ability, and the rationale to take up an extreme sport in the first place. While much of the book draws heavily on the equipment and techniques used by the competitive freediver, there is no intent to guide the reader in that direction. Neither is it the expectation that the reader has a background in competitive freediving.

Equally I considered using the term 'breath-hold diver', however this would then appear exclusive of those who are content to remain at the surface. For the purposes of this book, anyone who takes to the water with a pair of fins and a mask (but not scuba) has been termed a freediver.

Competitive freedivers use some fairly complex and demanding techniques to enable them to reach their depth objectives, but the ones explored here are some of the more fundamental and easy-to-grasp concepts. In the book there is more emphasis on performance, efficiency and safety, rather than strategies that aim to get someone as deep as possible for as long as possible. Throughout, there is the consideration that photography is the primary objective and the freediving insights are a tool to help you achieve better results within this realm.

Many snorkellers choose to remain at the surface. This can be due to personal preference, safety concerns, a medical condition or a physiological limitation such as blocked sinuses. For this group, some information (such as that in *Chapter 8: Neutral Buoyancy*) may be of academic interest only. The majority of the book will still be relevant though, and even *Chapter 9: Hydrodynamics* will provide insightful information. It is fairly simple to distinguish between the sections of the book that are applicable and those that are not.

In a similar manner, the advice and guidance that refers to stills photography applies by and large to videography. In fact, observing videographers underwater helped

Freediver using a GoPro video camera

mould the initial concept of this book. When watching the 'making of' tail sections of underwater documentaries, I sometimes observed camera operators filming while freediving. Their duration underwater was less than optimal, and poor technique and/or the wrong equipment was a significant contributing factor. Also, I am acutely aware that the emergence of extremely compact sized videographic equipment (for example GoPro) with the ability to record in 4k definition, is rapidly increasing in popularity. In addition, most modern digital cameras now have the ability to record video content. As with the snorkelling photographer, it should be straightforward enough in establishing the common ground.

A simple model I refer to as 'The Freediving Actualisation Triangle' is constructed from three fundamental elements. These are *equipment*, *technique* and *training*. The application of these three create the chance to transform oneself from a swimmer into a competent freediver. Should this in fact be a tetrahedron with a fourth element of *ability* added? My view is that it shouldn't. Ability is by and large  a product of training and technique. Of course some people do adapt better than others, but the significant gains that are there to be made emanate from the three aforementioned principles.

Throughout the book you will find that training is frequently encouraged. Technique is broken down into the various components, spread over several chapters. There is a single chapter devoted to freediving equipment, another to photographic equipment and one which covers basic underwater photography techniques.

I also acknowledge that there will be those that have specialist interests. One of my previous students enrolled for a course on underwater freediving photography, for the purpose of improving her ability to tag whale sharks. With a little tailoring, I was able to modify the course for her, and she was more than happy with the end result. Likewise, the information presented here can be read in context to the relevant activity. The only exclusions I can think of, are those that perform underwater imaging using pole systems, or from remotely operated vehicles (ROVs). These would require an entirely different set of skills.

One of my philosophies in life is to maximise the longevity of the tools I use. If I throw something away, then it really has stopped working. My main underwater camera is a Panasonic Micro Four Thirds system, one of the early models and several years old now. I bought it because it delivered the quality of image I was looking for, in a size that was appropriate for my freediving needs. Technology has since moved on and it would make my life so much easier if I now upgraded. But where would be the fun in that? When I can sit back and honestly tell myself that I am producing the best images possible with my camera, perhaps then I will upgrade.

As you go through this book and look at *my* images (the ones that show camera settings without a credit), you will see the result of this philosophy. The images that others and I have taken demonstrate the accompanying advice, and introduce each chapter. They also serve to show what is possible with freediving underwater photography. It is my hope that the reader will feel able to achieve the same or better with the appropriate training, equipment and experience.

There is one final point I would like to make. By far the most common reason I encounter from scuba divers who discount the possibility of learning to free-dive is that they feel they lack breath-hold ability. There are two enlightening aspects here that will help overcome any doubt. Firstly, it is easy to improve breath-holding fairly quickly. I have previously worked in the fast-paced tele-vision and film industry, where actors and presenters have needed to learn breath-hold techniques and learn them rapidly. Obtaining improvements of one hundred percent or more over a couple of hours was frequently possible. One BBC presenter achieved a breath-hold of over four minutes with a little coaching, and the world of competitive freediving would have been open to her had she chosen it.

The second aspect to this is that breath-hold technique is just one blade within a substantial freediving Swiss army knife. To open some of the others, please read on. To open all and sharpen them, please consider a freediving course.

Macro subjects are a challenge for the freediving photographer, but not an impossibility [Panasonic GF1 with 45mm lens, INON housing, single INON S2000 strobe, f5 at 1/160s, ISO 100]

Better equipped to keep up with the dolphins © Laura Storm/Planet Plankton
[Canon EOS 550D with 15mm lens, SEA&SEA housing, f7.1 at 1/640s, ISO 200]

Freediving Equipment for Underwater Photography

'It is with life just as with swimming; that man is the most expert who is the most disengaged from all encumbrances'

Apuleius[1]

Equipment is one of the fundamental elements of the Freediving Actualisation Triangle (FAT). It is not however the be-all and end-all. Some underwater photographers adopt the equipment and forego the techniques and training. In many cases this amounts to just a pair of freediving fins. This is a false economy, as the equipment can only deliver so much in the way of performance. Used incorrectly it can even be counter-productive.

Why purchase a pair of fins that cost more than a training course on how to use them? A better investment is an all-round one that addresses all of our FAT components. There *are* economies that can be made with equipment choices that minimise the impact on performance, and these will be discussed.

Combining the right equipment with the right training and technique does however, make a world of difference.

Fins

This section could be titled 'Bifins' or 'Stereo-fins' in order to distinguish these from the single-bladed monofin, favoured by the competitive freediver. The monofin is touched on in *Chapter 6: Finning* and *Chapter 9: Hydrodynamics*, and needs no further mention here. For an underwater photographer, the only interest would be where a freediving subject may be using one.

Freediving fins have a characteristic long, narrow blade in comparison to their scuba counterparts. The blade can be permanently fixed to the foot pocket, or detachable. The dimensions of the blade are such that maximum performance can be driven from the wearer.

---

1   Roman philosopher, rhetorician and satirist (124 AD–170 AD).

This brings about an interesting question: why aren't all fins (including those for scuba diving) shaped like this, if they maximise performance? It is simply down to practicality. Long-bladed fins make it more difficult to judge where the fin tips are, which could cause damage to the surroundings or the blades themselves. They are also more difficult to store and transport. Last but not least, they are normally 'closed heel' fins, whereas most scuba divers prefer the flexibility/ practicality of open heel fins so that neoprene boots can be worn. There is nothing to stop someone from using freediving fins to scuba dive.

Scuba vs. freediving fin

There are hybrid fins available that combine long blades with open heel pockets; these are designed for the spearfisher who may need to walk over rough terrain in neoprene boots. Whether there is much of a performance gain over open heel scuba fins is debatable.

Coming back to the closed heel design of freediving fins, this again is performance-related. Due to the integral construction, a snug-fitting pocket will be able to deliver much more torque from muscle to blade, than a foot that only has a strap connecting it to the fin around the back of the heel. The pocket does need to be a snug fit though, and if there is any looseness this can be counteracted by wearing neoprene socks. Additionally, a Y-shaped rubber 'fin keeper' which makes additional outside strapping of foot to pocket, can be beneficial.

Fin keeper securing foot to fin pocket

Performance can be tuned further by changing the stiffness, and most freediving fin manufacturers offer variable blades. The stiffer the blade, the more thrust that is delivered, but at the cost of more effort. For many people the stiff blades can be too tiring and may cause cramp. The benefit of being able to vary the stiffness of the blades is that performance tuning is at least possible, and the correct grade can be matched to the diver's physiology.

We now know that fin performance is achieved through design and shape, but there is another aspect to consider: composition. There are broadly speaking, three fin composites — thermoplastic polymer, fibreglass and carbon fibre.

Thermoplastic polymer fins have two main benefits — they are more robust and less expensive than fibreglass or carbon fibre. They are easy to source and many styles and colours are available. You can even buy a pair with clear blades if you wish! This type of fin is a sensible choice for the novice freediver, and will most likely still serve a useful purpose following any upgrade to either of the other composites.

Fibreglass fins are thinner and lighter than thermoplastic. They are also more expensive than thermoplastic, although cost less than carbon fibre. One of their benefits is that they are much more durable than carbon fibre, but less so than thermoplastic. Their lighter construction does deliver another benefit, which is better performance, however this is not as much as with carbon fibre. For price and durability they sit midway between the other two composites, but my own experience is that their performance is less than the halfway mark. In the world of competitive freediving, fibreglass bifins are rarely used.

Carbon fibre is the ultimate composite for freediving fins, and also the most expensive. It can be somewhat brittle, and a hard kick against a swimming pool wall might easily cause cracking or shattering. The reason it performs so well is that is has an elastic quality. If you bend back a thermoplastic fin with your hand and then release it, you will observe it snap back to its normal shape. Not so with carbon fibre. The blade will instead wane over into the opposing plane before resting centrally. While this is only a small degree of extra movement, it is enough to deliver a 'free' boost that is noticeable by comparison to a thermoplastic fin.

Due to the thinness of fibreglass and carbon fibre blades, a poorly executed kick can cause them to twist and slip sideways through the water. To minimise this, they have rubber or silicon side rails which act as stabilisers.

I mentioned earlier that just buying a pair of freediving fins on their own would be a false economy. If however, you were only prepared to buy one item of equipment to improve performance, a decent pair of fins would be the correct choice.

Wetsuit

The design of freediving wetsuits is very similar to that of scuba wetsuits from the 1960s and 1970s. Scuba wetsuits have evolved in design and material, whereas freediving wetsuits have evolved more in material and less in design. I think this is just a reflection of it working well for freediving purposes and not needing to change. Isn't it refreshing when that happens? How often do we bemoan a product that has evolved from something quite useful to something barely fit for purpose, seemingly for the sake of change?

Tailor-made two-piece freediving wetsuit with attached hood

Freediving wetsuits have a top and bottom (pants or leggings). The pants have a high waist and the top has an integrated hood. The top also has a tailpiece that extends from the back to pass under the crotch and is secured at the front. One of the advantages of this design is that the neoprene thickness is doubled for a generous band around the middle of the torso. The integrated hood also helps with streamlining.

The hood and doubled section of neoprene increase its thermal properties beyond that of a typical scuba wetsuit of an identical thickness. However, two other factors (if chosen) can add significantly more. If the material is 'open-cell' on the inside, it can cling to the skin to create a thermal barrier. The clinging property is also known as the 'suction effect'. This barrier is even more effective if the suit has been tailor-made for the individual. An off-the-peg suit will inevitably create pockets in the areas that don't quite fit, and these will fill with water. A tailor-made wetsuit of 3mm thickness is generally warmer than a 5mm off-the-peg unhooded one-piece scuba wetsuit. It also requires a lot less ballast to offset the positive buoyancy of the neoprene.

Why then don't scuba divers use freediving suits? First and foremost, the material (to be discussed shortly) is far too susceptible to rips and tears from hard/sharp scuba equipment. Also, given that there are no zips on freediving suits, the squeezing in and out takes a bit of practice and getting used to.

The neoprene material for freediving wetsuits needs to comprise several properties. The top three are water friction reduction, stretch ability (to allow deep breathing) and thermal protection. Much lower down the list, is durability. So if the chosen neoprene stretches well, slicks smoothly through the water and keeps one reasonably warm, then some durability may have to be sacrificed. Neoprene that acts as described will easily rip on a protruding nail or rough object, and may only last three or four years before it begins to deteriorate. Requirements may vary for the underwater photographer, depending on location. It could be that some external smoothness can be sacrificed for better durability if for example you are photographing in turbulent water near to rough terrain. Whatever your preference these variations can be achieved, but first we must examine the components of wetsuit neoprene.

Neoprene types tend to be classified by their manufacturer and optionally some other modifier. So a 'Yamamoto 45' is from manufacturer Yamamoto and is their number 45 compound, which is quite light and stretchy. Heiwa refers to a neoprene produced by the manufacturer of that name, which by comparison to Yamamoto 45 is denser but more durable and compresses less at depth. There are many others with many variations.

Earlier, I mentioned 'open-cell' neoprene. In fact this is a misnomer as all wetsuit neoprene consists of bubbles or 'closed cells' of nitrogen embedded within the rubber compound. When there is an internal lining present then that is termed 'closed-cell', and when there is no internal lining the open-cell definition is used. As an alternative to internal lining the inside layer can be coated, typically with titanium, so that body heat is reflected back. A coated inside layer often makes putting on the wetsuit an easier task.

On the outer layer, a smooth finish will achieve the friction reduction that many will want and benefit from. For those that require less vulnerability to snagging, then the outside can be lined with nylon or similar … but with reduced smoothness.

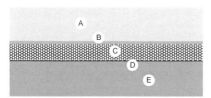

Neoprene cross-section — A: External air/water, B: Lining or finish, C: Neoprene (with nitrogen bubbles shown larger than actual), D: Inner coating, if applied, E: Freediver body tissue

The thermal benefit of an uncoated open-cell interior is offset by the potential difficulty in putting the wetsuit on. Some find it relatively easy, with perhaps just a splash of water spread inside the suit. Others need a little assistance in the form of a lubricant. Since neoprene is a rubber compound, oil should be avoided at all costs, as this will over time dissolve the material.

A lubricant, like a mild detergent or hair conditioner can be mixed with water (something along the lines of one part soap to ten parts water) and a few squirts used to coat the inside of the suit. It is good to be mindful of the impact on the environment, and whenever possible not use excessive amounts of detergent. Better still, is to use something more ecologically friendly. There is an interesting food additive called 'carageenan' which is supplied in the form of powder, and which when water is added mixes into a gel. It is extracted from seaweeds and mosses and makes a great environmentally friendly lubricant.

One alternative that can be considered to a conventional two-piece freediving wetsuit, is a triathlon suit and swimming cap. Some competitive freedivers prefer these for situations where they are doing more exertion (for example not using fins at all). Not having a hood and being single thickness, the thermal insulation is less by comparison. I view the use of these for the underwater photographer as more of a 'make-do' alternative. If you already have one and don't want to spend money on another wetsuit, then in the right environment a triathlon suit can work. A typical single-piece 3/5mm combination suit will be less warm than a two-piece 3mm freediving wetsuit, so that's worth bearing in mind.

Mask

If you have looked into the pricing of carbon fibre fins and tailor-made wetsuits, you could be wondering where the term 'freediving' came from. You may be pleasantly surprised to find out that face masks for freediving are a little more reasonable.

The main distinction with a freediving mask is that it should be low profile and low volume. The mask should not protrude significantly from the face, otherwise it interferes with the flow of water (explored in *Chapter 9: Hydrodynamics*). Low volume can also be important, depending on what depth you plan to dive to. At a depth of ten metres, the ambient pressure doubles and compressible air spaces therefore halve in volume. The mask's air space will have halved in volume, and to replace this the only available air must come from your lungs in order to 'equalise' the air space. So the larger the mask volume, the more air you will lose from your lungs to compensate for any loss due to depth pressure.

Scuba divers also benefit from low profile masks, but low volume is less useful (although the two attributes are normally combined). This is because scuba divers' lungs do not compress at depth, which is due to them receiving air at ambient pressure.

Some freediving masks are little more than swimming goggles with an integrated nosepiece to allow for air compensation. Some of them have curved and/or plastic lenses, which are fine for competitive freedivers, but not for underwater photographers. A flat glass lens is preferable if using a camera. The low profile quality of the mask is more applicable

Typical low-volume low-profile mask suitable for freediving

to the underwater photographer than the low volume. Higher volume masks are only really a problem at greater depths where the lungs become unable to pass air back to the head. This is unlikely to be a depth where most freediving photographers will venture to.

Snorkel

As with the facemask, simple and inexpensive are the key attributes. A simple 'J' shaped design with all-round rigidity is all that is required. Snorkels with soft corrugated 'U' bends are better suited for scuba divers, not freedivers. They do not function unless strapped to the mask, and many freedivers prefer not to do this. If you do attach the snorkel to your mask, then you will either a) remove it before descending, or b) leave it attached for the dive. Removing and replacing a corrugated snorkel is more cumbersome compared to a rigid one, and it creates more drag underwater. So it benefits neither case for the freediver.

Some snorkels have purge valves near the mouthpiece, but this is another feature less useful for freediving. A purge valve encourages the freediver to expel water with lung air at the end of a dive. A surfacing freediver should be taking their first exhalation and inhalation with their head clear of the water and mouth away from the snorkel (as explained in *Chapter 7: Descents and Ascents*). Most water will drain of its own accord and any remainder can be manually tipped out.

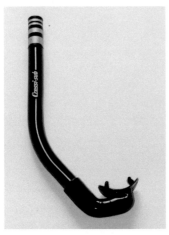

For freedivers leaving snorkels mask-attached, for safety reasons the mouthpiece should not really be in the mouth during a dive. Not all freedivers find this convenient, and not all adhere to this advice. If you look closely throughout the book, you will find one or two images where snorkels were not removed from freedivers' mouths, which was the personal choice of the freediver concerned at that time and situation. This is not a representation of my own view, which remains that any mask-attached snorkel should be outside of the mouth during a freedive.

Snorkel type suitable for freediving

One variation that can be useful, is a tube that arches around the head (instead of a straight tube). It makes the snorkel more hydrodynamic if left mask-attached during a dive.

Weight Belt and Weights

The most popular type of weight belt for the freediver is a plain rubber strip with perforations that passes through a square buckle. This is known as a Marseillaise belt.

The belt needs to be made of rubber rather than the webbing type favoured by scuba divers, so that it can contract at depth and not slip around the torso. Fastening the belt tightly at the surface ensures that it stays where it should.

The belt should be worn on the hips rather than the waist. If you have invested in a pliable, stretchy wetsuit that allows deep, abdominal breathing; then a weight belt causing a restriction around the waist counteracts this ability.

The design of a Marseillaise belt enables it to be quickly released in an emergency. If the loose end is pulled away from the buckle, the centre prong pops out of its perforation to allow the free end to slide back through. When you are wearing the belt, to prevent the free end flapping around, a section can be folded and tucked under the main loop around the hips. That way a much smaller free end is left, and when pulled will release the tucked-away section just before activating the main release. For safety's sake do not pass the free end under the primary loop without folding, otherwise pulling the free end will have no effect.

Marseillaise belt correctly worn and undergoing quick-release

Marseillaise belts can carry scuba weights, as long as the weights haven't become distorted so that the threading slot is too narrow, as the belt is a few millimetres thicker than a scuba webbing belt. These sorts of issues can normally be resolved with some tools at the dive shop, but possibly not out at sea. Check your weight situation *before* setting sail.

Socks and Gloves

Apart from keeping your feet warm, neoprene socks will help prevent any rubbing with fin pockets on backs of heels. They can also help with fin efficiency as described earlier.

Gloves for freediving are no different to those used by scuba divers. Make sure you don't use a new pair of gloves for the first time on a photographic expedition. You need to be comfortable with operating the controls on your housing with the gloves you intend to use. Therefore practising beforehand makes sense.

Both gloves and socks come in 3mm or 5mm thicknesses, most commonly. There are some odd thicknesses slightly lower and higher, but the 3–5mm range is likely to be most suitable.

Dive Computer

A dive computer offering freediving (or 'gauge') mode, is an important if not essential piece of equipment. Some dive computer manufacturers provide computers dedicated to freediving, and most are able to offer computers that are compatible for both scuba and freediving.

In freediving mode it is fairly standard to have a time display, temperature, depth, time submerged, and dive interval time. Also alarms for specific depths and/or times. All of these provide useful information for the freediver.

Knowing your depth is useful for a variety of reasons, one of which is establishing a neutrally buoyant point. You can take an initial dive to establish where this is, and use the computer on subsequent dives to maintain a depth near to but above the prescribed depth.

Dive computer in freediving mode

When you are concentrating on your photography it is all too easy to lose track of your submerged time. The dive computer provides an essential reference point.

The dive interval time is also particularly important. You will have an established minimum, based on your physiology, previous dive time, and overall maximum number of dives for a given time span. When surfacing, the computer detects this and records a single dive. This allows you to monitor your time between separate dives.

If you find yourself chilly in your wetsuit and you need a thicker one, obviously you'll also want to know at what temperature that was and your computer can provide that information.

One important point to note with freediving computers or modes is that they cannot at time of writing assess nitrogen loading into your fluids and tissues. Scuba modes can, so this is a primary functional difference. Not knowing this information is one of the reasons that mixing scuba and freediving is unknown territory, and should therefore be avoided.

Diver's Float

The use of the diver's float is covered at various points in the book so here it will only be described in brief. It is an extremely useful and important accessory however, hence the repeated references.

In its most basic form a float can consist of an inflated plastic tube, ring or bag; used for support before and after dives. Additional adaptations can further the functionality. If it is of a sturdy construction (such as an inflated car inner tube contained within a strong canvas cover), then a weighted guide line can be attached to the underside, provided an attachment point is present. Again, if the construction includes a covered tube, the covering can have a top opening into which snorkels and other equipment may be deposited.

Underside of a freediving float

Attaching a diver's flag is straightforward enough, and one of the most sensible precautions a pair of freedivers can take to improve visibility to surrounding marine traffic. This can also act as a visual reference to a boat captain who may have transported you.

With a little extra rigging, a decent float setup can be converted into a Submersible Optics Underwater Platform Assembly, or 'SOUPA'. This can be used to deploy camera equipment from surface to depth, and is another equipment topic described and illustrated in *Chapter 7: Descents and Ascents*.

Accessories

There are no end of other bits and bobs you can take along on your dive trips. Some of the more important to consider are the safety-related items such as a whistle. In *Chapter 10: Safety* you will find information about the FRV — the Freediver's Recovery Vest. This is definitely worth considering. A bottle of water is a good idea and one sometimes overlooked, as well as sunscreen and a hat.

For the freediving itself, I have seen underwater scooters used before, but rarely observed this combined with underwater photography. It is more task-loading, but could work with enough organisation and practice. There would be the opportunity for some creative motion blur images, perhaps. It is also a neat solution to transport you from A to B when a boat is unable to. With the right navigation and used fully submerged, it is a fairly quick way to arrive at your destination with a lot less effort. Your photographic configuration will have a bearing on whether one of these is useful or not.

Whatever you decide to take, bear in mind that if you don't need it while submerged, then leave it attached to or inside the float. A waterproof MP3 player might bring a new dimension to your freediving experience, but that dimension will not be streamlining.

Underwater scooter mobility

Summary

The more expensive items of equipment are fins, wetsuit and dive computer. In contrast, most of the other items are fairly reasonably priced. Increasing spend on freediving equipment is like any other investment though — wisely researched you should end up with better quality and functionality. For your wetsuit this can make the difference between keeping warm and being cold. Some key points on equipment:

- Choose between thermoplastic, fibreglass and carbon fibre for fin composition.
- A tailor-made wetsuit will deliver superior performance and insulation.
- Avoid masks with curved or plastic lenses and look for a low-profile design.
- Leave corrugated snorkels for scuba divers and choose a rigid one.
- New gloves need testing before use in the field.
- A dive computer can be dedicated to freediving or a scuba/freediving hybrid.
- A canvas covered car tyre inner tube offers adaptation potential.
- Prioritise safety accessories above those of convenience or entertainment.

2

Freediver with housed camera set up for natural light image capture
[Panasonic GF1 with 7-14mm lens, INON housing, f10 at 1/80s, ISO 400]

Photographic Equipment

'For most of us, cameras and underwater housings are just a means to an end'
Paul Colley[1]

For those readers unfamiliar with underwater photographic equipment, this chapter will be a useful starting point and I hope will whet your appetite for further research. You may be surprised to find only one chapter each devoted to the subjects of photographic equipment and technique (*Chapter 3: Underwater Photography Basics*). There are entire volumes written by others on both these subjects, which is partly the point — this book is mainly about how to freedive better in order to enable a long enough breath-hold to take decent photos. For the experienced underwater photographers among you, there is some useful information on techniques and adaptations that relate to freediving in *Chapter 4: Challenges and Opportunities for Freedivers*.

There are two sections in this chapter. The first is a reclassification of the confusing emergence of overlapping imaging options, into simple categories. This leads on to the second section — a breakdown of the other components that transform the camera into an underwater imaging system.

The identification of particular models of equipment has been largely avoided. This is partly because photographic equipment is positioned in a fast-moving market with changes frequent and developments rapid.

Camera Options — A Simple Classification

The Three-part Model

Let us firstly look at three significant factors that come into play when we decide what we want to achieve with an underwater digital camera investment.

The CCD (charge-coupled device), more commonly known as the 'sensor', is a good starting point. Although the sensor isn't the exclusive determination

---

1   *Winning Images with Any Underwater Camera: The Essential Guide to Creating Engaging Photos* (2014) Oxford: Dived Up Publications.

of image quality, it is arguably the most fundamental. This is the point where the image information is captured, and the larger the surface area the more information that can be stored. This should not be confused with the resolution capacity in megapixels. The pixels that are stored in files on the media card are derived from the information in the sensor, and it is not necessarily a one-to-one mapping! Therefore **high pixel counts with a given sensor size will not yield a significantly better image quality than an alternative with fewer pixels and the same sized sensor**.

The lens is another quality-defining factor in our investment equation. It channels and focuses light onto the sensor, and may be fixed or interchangeable. Interchangeable lenses provide the flexibility to have a broad range of distances from which we can capture images (but are not interchangeable when we are under or within water). A fixed lens may also have a fairly wide range, but even the best will not be able to match the potential performance and quality from an interchangeable lens camera.

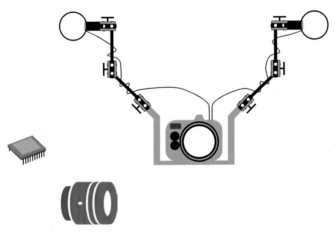

From left to right: sensor, lens and final assembly.
Qualitative, qualitative, and quantitative

The last factor to be considered is the external dimensions of the camera once transformed into an underwater system. For some current compact systems there may be no transformation necessary, if they are sufficiently waterproof at the depth you intend to use them (and the manufacturer states that they will remain so). For most though, the camera will need to be housed in a waterproof case and there are various optional accessories which can be added to these. The end result will be a system (or 'rig') of a certain size. That size may be larger than you'd ideally like for efficient freediving performance.

The first two factors affect the third. Cameras with interchangeable lenses are generally larger than those with inbuilt fixed lenses. Cameras with larger sensors tend to have larger external dimensions than those with smaller sensors, although recent developments have seen large sensors installed into small camera bodies. To summarise everything so far, better quality images are likely to mean larger and more expensive camera systems. Before we look at how to choose the right configuration, we need to look at some way of simplifying the myriad of options that exist.

Equipment and Basics

Four Form Systems

I'll use some self-styled terminology here, just within the confines of this publication. The aim is to position camera systems into different sized 'forms', and provision four of these. They are *Small Form, Medium Form, Large Form,* and *Oversize Form.* Because camera manufacturers now vary sensor sizes between the different types of camera, we will ignore sensor size when considering the different forms. (This doesn't mean sensor size should be ignored when assessing a purchase; in fact it should be one of the primary considerations!).

Medium form in use

Small Form comprises compact cameras with inbuilt fixed lenses (which may be able to zoom, but still termed 'fixed' as they are not removable). They can be carried with one hand, even when housed with accessory parts added.

Medium Form includes cameras that have interchangeable lenses, but excludes all but the smallest single lens reflex (or 'mirrored' systems). Some digital SLRs are small enough to fit into lower profile housings and take up no more space than a 'mirrorless' system. If the housed system with no accessories can still be carried in one hand, it can be considered medium form. For the non-digital enthusiasts, mirrorless film cameras will also be included here.

Large form shown in use by freediver on the left,
and small form by the one on the right

Large Form systems are the majority of SLRs. Something that when housed, really needs two hands to safely carry. Mirrorless systems may also be positioned here, if sufficient accessory addition has meant they cannot be carried with one hand.

Oversize Form relates to specialist stills equipment and large scale videographic equipment. This would be something that probably needs more than one person to handle out of the water. There are seasoned professionals around who can freedive with oversize form, but they are few and far between. This book considers sizes that go up to and include large form, when referring to freediving with them. Oversize form freediving needs specialist consideration on a case-by-case basis.

Oversize form in use © Sue Flood, Tartan Dragon Ltd

Pre-Acquisition Process

Having looked at size classification, should a system be chosen based on this? Personally, I would go back to the first two of the three decision factors discussed earlier (sensor and lens choice in terms of fixed vs. interchangeable), and then attempt to position the outcome into the third (form size) that is most appropriate for the expected usage. This could then be viewed as a possible configuration, to which you then apply other deciding factors. These will be features associated with the camera body, such as the ability to shoot raw, manual white balance, battery life, and many others. Also, you may have an existing equipment investment to consider, and wish to reuse strobes, lenses and other accessories. Determining all of these factors may be a cyclical process whereby the end result fails to match all requirements, and you need to start again. We all have our own ways of deciding on a piece of equipment to invest in, but if you find yourself getting lost you could try the approach I have described here.

The primary requirement should really be the end product. If you are new to underwater photography, and want to impress your friends on Facebook with underwater images you have captured while freediving (and why not?!), then large form may be overkill. Conversely, if you have been commissioned by *National Geographic* to do an underwater feature in Antarctica, then a small form configuration might not deliver good enough quality for publication.

Let's take a third, hypothetical example and work it through. You have an existing small form configuration and you wish to upgrade. You want to produce images that can win competitions, both digitally viewed and in print. Your primary income doesn't come from photography. You quite like the idea of freediving, and want a setup that works well for this. The starting point here could be to look at cameras with interchangeable lenses and as large a sensor as possible, and see what the housed result would look like. If it ends up being large form, is there an alternative consideration that results in medium form? If there is, will it still be able to deliver images of the quality you require? Clearly there are many other questions to be answered here. The answer could even be an upgrade from one small form system to another, as there are many of these that can produce competition-winning results (with the right photographic techniques of course!).

If you haven't already discovered this, when you assemble an underwater imaging system, the cost of everything (if buying new) other than the camera body is far greater than the camera itself. If you are on a tight budget, then purchasing used equipment is one option. You may also want to consider a backup camera body. If your primary camera becomes damaged, then you won't have lost your housing investment as well.

Many readers will have already made an investment in a camera system, and may now wonder if they need something different for freediving, especially if what they have now is large form. I wouldn't advise going down that route unless an insurmountable problem is encountered with the current configuration, or an upgrade is being considered anyway. There are many freediving photographers who handle the large form quite successfully, and the equipment and techniques detailed in this book will complement the ability to cope.

Housing
When preparing to take your camera underwater, the first step is fairly obvious. It needs to be waterproof! Mentioned in brief earlier, some 'amphibious' cameras are waterproof at the outset. A number of these tend to be only for a couple of metres depth and beyond that the water pressure exceeds the camera's ability to resist water penetration. I'm not convinced that regular underwater usage of this type of camera without further protection is a good idea, especially in salt water. When salt water evaporates, salt crystals are left behind and these can accumulate

in parts of the camera beyond your reach. This could cause moving parts to stick, and others to corrode. Many waterproof cameras can be protected in the same way as their non-waterproof counterparts, i.e. with a case, or housing. For low-cost alternatives there are waterproof bag systems available as well, but make sure you can actuate all controls if you opt for something of this nature. Also note that they are only really useful at or very near to the surface as they provide little or no protection to the camera against increasing water pressure.

A housing is essentially a waterproof box that encases your camera. It can be produced by the camera manufacturer, or more commonly by a specialist housing manufacturer. There is a chasing game to be played when considering one of the latter. If you purchase a brand new model of camera, there may not yet be a housing available for it, at least not from a manufacturer of your preference. If you were to purchase a housing first, then the camera it has been designed for may have been withdrawn from retail. You need to find a sweet spot where both an up-to-date camera of your choice and a

A coated aluminium under-
water camera housing

housing from a manufacturer of your choice are both readily available. This is why most underwater camera retail outlets will supply packages that include both elements.

One combination to be wary of is a new model of camera with a housing from a less-reputable manufacturer. Not all housing manufacturers test their products to the same level of stringency. You don't really want to find yourself the owner of a MK1 model of housing, when three months later the MK2 is the one where the leaking problem has been resolved.

Housings can be found in all types of materials from polyurethane, flexible PVC and aluminium to a variety of polycarbonates. There are various rods, levers, buttons and dials that move from the outer to the inner casing, and these actuate the various camera buttons. If you have a camera with interchangeable lenses, then there is normally an interchangeable front port to the housing as well, which matches to the lens being used. If you are likely to add an external 'wet' conversion lens, then make sure there is a compatible thread or other connection method on the outside of the housing front port.

A final housing component is the strobe interface. This is either to allow electronic signals to effectively pass through the case, or a window to allow light from the camera flash to pass into an optical cable.

Housing Add-ons

The tray or base is a flat plate that the housing attaches to, and which will probably have one or two handles. It facilitates the attachment of strobe arms, meaning that it is only really necessary if you are using strobe lighting. Sometimes though, a firm base with a handle can be beneficial in its own right.

Strobe arms connect one or more strobes to the tray. Arms with balled ends are quite popular, as they allow movement in multiple planes. Arm sections can be latticed, cylindrical or tubular. The cylindrical sections are often filled with air or foam to provide buoyancy. This property can work against the objectives of the freediver, whereas arms with thin diameter tubes work toward. This is discussed in *Chapter 9: Hydrodynamics* in more detail.

Most arms, certainly those with balled ends, need something to connect one ball to another. This is a simple ball joint clamp, which uses a wing nut to tighten the clamp onto two or more adjoining balled ends.

The final elements of the configuration are the strobes. The deeper a person dives, the less light that makes its way down. Different wavelengths of light fade out before others, so that reds and yellows disappear much sooner than blues and greens. Even though there may be sufficient light for a correct exposure, it will be heavily cast in blue and/or green if taken at depth. There are different ways of dealing with this; the most popular is the strobe (the diver's name for a flash unit). By introducing a brief flash of electronic light, full colours are restored and a wider variety of camera settings can be used to control the image being captured (due to the increased amount of light). Contrast also increases due to this extra light.

External strobes are triggered from the camera flash, and a cable from housing to strobe achieves this. Some strobes do now have wireless activation.

Once extended, strobe arms can increase the overall dimensions of the rig quite considerably. From a photographic perspective, this is desirable in order to make some distance between lens and light source. Too close and *backscatter* can be a problem (see *Chapter 3: Underwater Photography Basics*). From a freediving perspective, extended strobe arms will create drag, slow the operator down, and in turn reduce his or her time underwater. It isn't something that has to be avoided at all cost, but it does need to be considered.

Housing with accessories attached

To further add to the structure there are focusing lights, lanyards plus clips, external conversion lenses and external lens carriers to be considered as options. For the flying underwater photographer who is a scuba diver, the challenge is staying below the maximum baggage allowance; for the freediver it is overcoming the increased drag incurred.

Summary

The ideal camera for the freediving photographer is the one that produces the image (or footage) and quality that they wish to achieve. If the dimensions of this introduce a challenge with handling ability, then advice in the remainder of this book will introduce techniques to help overcome that. This chapter covered:

- Introduction of the three-part model: sensor, lens and external dimensions.
- Consideration of the four forms: small, medium, large and oversize.
- Taking a realistic view of image quality actually required when choosing an imaging package.
- Being wary of new camera models in housings of unknown quality.
- The more accessories added, the more water resistance will be encountered.

3

Easily approachable fish in shallow water, such as this black grouper,
are the perfect opportunity to practice basic photography skills
[Panasonic GF1 with 7-14mm lens and INON housing, f8 at 1/160s, ISO 200]

Underwater Photography Basics **3**

'My camera can and I will!'
Martin Edge[1]

If you buy an underwater camera system and then use it for the first time without researching the basic techniques, you will almost certainly be disappointed. Having said that, sometimes it isn't easy to appreciate your own shortcomings until you look at the work of more accomplished photographers. I have to put my hands up here and say that this realisation took me a lot longer than it should have! It is very easy to marvel at a fuzzy blue image of something tiny within a mass of greyish snow when you know that it was taken on a special encounter you experienced. Friends you show this to could be quietly unimpressed and you may never know.

In this chapter I will relay a few points on underwater photography that will make a significant difference if you are a beginner. For a more in-depth approach there are other books dedicated to underwater photography technique.[2]

The very first thing to do, is learn and practice your chosen discipline that enables the photography, i.e. freediving. If you are not comfortable in the underwater environment (and you only will be from practice and training), then you won't have the ability to cope effectively with both diving processes and photography when combined. For the same reason it is also important to learn how to use your camera and all the functions you may need underwater.

Technique

Very high on your list of priorities should be getting as close as possible to your subject. There is a simple reason for this; the behaviour of light within water means that subjects will lose colour and contrast much more dramatically as

---

1   *The Underwater Photographer* (4th Edn., 2010) Oxford: Focal Press.
2   An invaluable all-round book on underwater photography is Martin Edge's aforementioned *The Underwater Photographer*. For more on putting together artistically pleasing images see Paul Colley's *Winning Images with Any Underwater Camera* (2014) Oxford: Dived Up Publications.

they become more distant from the lens. For live and dynamic subjects you need to make an approach that doesn't frighten them off, and not chase. For large static objects where this is not an issue, you may still be too far away for your lens to fit everything in. This is where a wide-angle lens pays dividends. If you are using a small form system, then you will hopefully have an attachment point on the front port of your camera housing where you can add a conversion wide-angle lens. This addition alone can help you achieve a noticeable improvement in the quality of your images, when combined with the act of getting closer to the subject.

This dolphin image (yes, it is a dolphin!) has many faults, and has been taken at a distance of around three metres, in poor light on a small form system without a wide-angle attachment or strobe.

This image is somewhat better, taken in good light on a medium form system with a wide-angle lens, and without strobe. The lens allowed me to get much closer, and the main improvements are due to quality of light and proximity to subject.

Balancing Colour

Getting close to the subject will not significantly change the overall colour balance brought about by the characteristics of light through water (loss of colours from the spectrum at increasing depth and horizontal distance through the water column), certainly not with the background. To solve this there are five potential solutions:

1. Shoot in *raw* mode (if your camera has this feature). Raw shooting is more or less a 'dump' of all the information on the sensor into a file, with no processing or loss of data. So it enables post-processing on a computer to alter amongst other things the white balance. You should be able to pick out something in the image that has blue/green tones where it would normally be white or grey. The software can then normalise the white balance based on an area you click.[3] If you try this on a jpeg image, there is less information to work with and the outcome can be variable. Even with raw files it occasionally doesn't work well, but for ambient light imagery above fifteen metres, results tend to be good.

2. Use *manual white balance*. This is again, if your camera has the feature. This is where a sample is taken at a given depth and light condition, of a neutral test point (as white as possible). The camera then makes the white balance correction on-board in real time, rather than with post-processing as in the previous case.

3. Use *correction filters*. These can be external or applied inside the housing, depending on the type chosen. External filters are threaded discs with a coloured lens that screw on to the front of the lens port. Internal filters tend to be coloured gel strips that are applied to the camera lens within the housing / port assembly. For the price of a small loss of light, the wavelengths are adapted so that the dominant blues and greens are 'held back' and the reds and yellows allowed through. That's on over-simplification, but approximates to how it works.

---

3   This is possible in industry-leading software like Adobe® Lightroom® and Photoshop® as well as alternative programs, which are often bundled with cameras by manufacturers. The specifics vary by app and software now evolves faster than cameras — consult your image processing app's 'Help' document.

4. Use *strobe(s)* to produce artificial light from a source much closer to your subject.
5. Convert the image from colour to *monochrome*. Perhaps more of an alternative than a solution, but it can rescue something you may otherwise have deleted.

Raw Slowdown

Shooting in raw has many positives, but it makes for large files, and can cause a time lag as the data is written to the memory card — the camera and storage media capabilities determine how long. So shooting raw may not be an acceptable approach for all camera configurations, even where the feature exists, because data write times may be too excessive to allow capture of 'peak-of-action' moments.

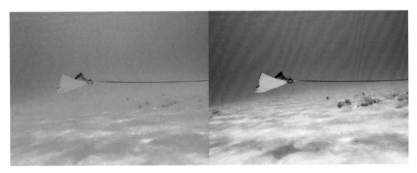

Image captured in raw mode before processing, and afterwards with white balance adjustment.

Exposure Controls

A seemingly appealing option with most cameras, is to allow the electronics to automatically capture an image with the correct exposure. There are usually 'priority' settings where you are allowed to adjust one setting, such as shutter speed or aperture. For systems with increased functionality you have the addition of a completely manual mode. Underwater, light levels are reduced overall, and certain wavelengths are absorbed more quickly than others. This won't affect the camera's ability to correctly expose an image when in an automated mode, but it can mean that the image does not appear quite how you envisaged it. The focus may not be sharp enough, or the background not the right colour. The only really effective way to create an image the way you envisage is to use a manual exposure programme (if your camera has the feature). This isn't a hard-and-fast rule, sometimes conditions are so changeable that a semi-automated priority setting is more flexible. Using manual mode will help you better understand the rules of exposure, and give you more flexibility with the outcome. This is really, 'try it and see' advice. If you do use manual exposure, you will find that other features on your camera can help you with the task. Some cameras for example will have a light meter display that overlays onto the LCD and provides exposure information. This is help you will need!

Rules of Exposure

Correct exposure is primarily governed by the different settings of shutter speed, aperture (or f-stop), and the ISO (sensitivity setting of the sensor). In manual mode these can all be varied independently, to create a desired level of exposure. Using priority modes, either the aperture or shutter speed can be altered, and the camera will change the other settings to create an exposure it calculates to be correct.

Unfortunately, our eyes are a poor judge of correct exposure, and what we see on the LCD screen may be something of an illusion. One issue is that the light from the LCD has to travel between a layer of glass or plastic (i.e. the housing), and then another of water before it hits the eye. More importantly though, our eyes are continually adjusting to the light around us, and this will influence what we see on the LCD screen. A good experiment is to take a manually exposed underwater shot in shallow water on a bright, sunny day. Preferably where the bottom is light and/or sandy. Using the LCD display, change the settings until (when reviewing the image) it appears that you have the correct exposure. Back on dry land, remove the camera from the housing and review the same image in a dimly lit room. You may be surprised at what you see. I would expect that you will find the image to be over-exposed.

There are a number of features that most cameras have to assist with this problem. Some have a scaled light meter that can be shown on the display at the time of shooting. Most have a 'highlights' feature that you can activate in review mode. This will cause pixels that are incorrectly exposed to flash on the display. Again in review mode, many cameras can show a histogram. This is the feature that I find most useful, but it does require a little research and understanding. If your camera has none of these features, or you feel it is over-complicating your way of photography, then manual exposure may be something to experiment with at a later date.

A histogram is split into the set of primary colours that are recorded on the sensor: red, green and blue (shown in the top right quadrant in the example picture). The plots represent how many pixels have been recorded for different exposure levels. To the left of each histogram the darkest pixels are recorded, and to the right are the lightest. The

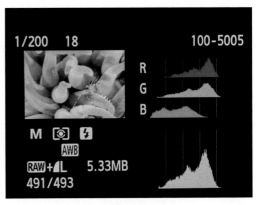

LCD Histogram

histogram in the lower right quadrant shows the combined colour values, and thus gives a useful indicator of overall exposure.

Backscatter

When using strobes, your biggest frustration is likely to be 'backscatter'. The first time I encountered this, I thought there was something wrong with the camera. It is where you can see lots of snow-like spots in the darker parts of your image. These shapes are no coincidence, as they are caused by tiny particles suspended in the water bouncing light from the strobe back to the camera (like tiny mirrors). It tends to be worse when the main beam of the strobe angles toward the subject, and is also quite close to the lens.

In very poor water conditions you often have no way of completely eliminating this. Moving the strobe further away from the lens helps. Angling the strobe outward a little, so that the 'hot' part of the beam is out of the shot, is also beneficial. Changing camera and/or strobe settings so that a better balance of ambient light is included, rather than mainly strobe light, is also a useful deterrent.

These few hints are really just the tip of the iceberg. There are many other fundamental improvement techniques that will also make a difference. My perspective is that the ones detailed here will make that difference positive and significant. Other improvement aspects that can be explored are composition, varying depth-of-field, advanced lighting options and post-production techniques.

Backscatter evident as various sized greyish circles in the background

Summary

This chapter has just skimmed the surface of an extensive subject. In doing so, the aim was to introduce the novice underwater photographer to a few simplifications and key ideas.

- Reduce distance to subject and correct white balance for superior results.
- Experiment with manual exposure mode if available.
- When using strobe, determine the best position to avoid backscatter.

Equipment and Basics

4

Photographer assessing subject and subject assessing photographer
© Laura Storm/Planet Plankton
[Canon EOS 550D with 15mm lens, SEA&SEA housing, f4 at 1/80s, ISO 200]

Challenges and Opportunities for Freedivers

'Luck is where opportunity meets preparation'
Denzel Washington

W hen considering the relationship between your photography equipment and the activity that achieves the photographic outcome (in this case freediving), there will be some limitations to be aware of, and adaptations may be necessary. Equally though, you will be better placed to grasp certain opportunities beyond the capabilities of the scuba diver.

Equipment and Basics

Deep Water Benefits and Issues

The term 'deep water' I will apply to whatever depth is reachable for you, but where you would only be able to stay for a few seconds before needing to return to the surface. We'll assume that there would be enough bottom time to compose and capture an image. Another assumption is that the subject is at depth (subjects in shallow water are looked at later in the chapter).

As long as you are in clear water, then being predominantly surface-based you have a wide panoramic view of what is beneath. There will also be fewer obstacles between you and a potential subject, compared to those between the subject and a photographer based near the bottom. For locating medium and larger sized subjects in the distance, you will have the advantage. For the tinier shrimp-sized subjects you are at a disadvantage.

These advantages and disadvantages will influence your lens choice. For those that have the option of interchangeability, a common choice in deep water will be a wide-angle lens. These frame a broader view of the subject and make it appear smaller (through the lens) in the LCD or viewfinder. This means that seascapes, shipwrecks and other larger subjects common in deep water are appropriate for wide-angle lens work. If however you attach a macro lens and then enter deep water, your biggest challenge would be locating something small. If you were able to do that, it would most likely mean an ascent to the surface for air before returning to photograph. That may well mean locating the subject again.

Is there a possible adaptation that would help in this situation? You could exploit your panoramic spotting ability from the surface, and locate something interesting of medium/large size. Perhaps something approachable with interesting patterns on its skin — a bluespotted stingray for example. Armed with your macro lens, you could descend and capture a close-up abstract image of the blue spots against the bronze background of the skin. Head portraits of larger fish are also an option.

Sand divers are medium-sized benthic dwelling fish; not difficult to locate, and their skin can make an interesting macro abstract

Shallow Water Benefits and Issues

Reading the above, you should be able to guess one of the benefits of shallow water. Macro photography of small subjects becomes a lot more practical, at least when the bottom is shallow as well. In this chapter the term 'shallow water' means in relation to you and the camera, not necessarily the depth of the bottom.

If shallow water means you have little or no descent to consider, and if the same applies to the distance to swim underwater, then drag becomes much less of a concern. This opens up much more flexibility with the use of strobes (although ironically the need to use them for wide-angle imagery in well-lit shallows diminishes). You also have less cause for concern about the overall size of your photographic equipment.

Shallow water underwater photography can very often take place in quite deep water. There are no end of subjects to be found in the top five metre zone: everything from sailfish to whales, jellyfish, flotsam, bait balls, basking sharks and more. This is where freediving photography really comes into its own. The scuba diver has multiple limitations working in this zone. Pressure change ratios are at their highest here, and a scuba diver continually bobbing up and down from the surface to the five to ten metres zone, risks decompression sickness issues. In particular, if they have residual nitrogen already in their tissues. Scuba divers are also a lot less manoeuvrable with all the equipment they have to carry. For photographing marine creatures in this top layer, freediving provides the key advantage.

Shallow water photography does pose one or two limitations on the freediver as well. Due to changes in pressure ratios previously mentioned, finding neutral buoyancy can be problematic. This problem can be worked around — *Chapter 8: Neutral Buoyancy* is devoted to the subject.

Camera housing with viewfinder (black circular eyepiece at top of back plate)

Another issue can arise when the sun is out in full force and the camera does not have a viewfinder (i.e. LCD back screen only). The force of the glare can make the screen difficult to view. For camera systems with a viewfinder, composing will not be affected by glare issues, but reviewing will be subject to them. Glare isn't easy to deal with but it can be mitigated. The brightness of the LCD is adjustable on most cameras, and increasing this may help. If you are reviewing an image rather than composing, another option is to dive underwater a few metres, if the depth is available. The water column will filter out some of the sun's intensity. If you have a towel carried within your float system, putting this over your head and camera can help as well.

Finally, a last opportunity to consider in shallow water photography is underwater surface reflection. In calm waters, some amazing reflections can be captured alongside the primary subject. If the freediver is positioned just a little below the surface, an upward angle can then capture both subject and reflection.

Interesting reflections in a shallow water image

The Strobe Issue

This is something which is referred to at various points within the book and the freediver's enemy is water resistance. In shallow water resistance is less of a concern. So we should not eliminate the idea of using strobes, far from it. Strobes can pose drag issues and are therefore sometimes abandoned, but there are adaptations that can assist.

Thinking about macro photography again, many macro images seem virtually impossible to capture without strobe. Small creatures frequently avoid detection in dark recesses. Also, at the levels of magnification used in macro, a lot of the image will be out of focus unless a small aperture (high f-stop) is used to provide a greater depth of field. This reduces light arriving on the sensor, and counteracting this is a reason strobes are used.

One adaptive possibility is to use the onboard flash. This will depend on the housing, particles in the water and a number of other factors. It is more likely to be feasible with small form cameras in housings where the flash lighting is

Equipment
and Basics

allowed to pass through. There is a higher risk of backscatter, but it may be minimal or absent if conditions are good and you are lucky.

Another option is possible for subjects that are out in the open. By opening up the aperture (low f-stop), you will allow extra ambient light onto the sensor and bring about a very narrow zone of focus. This can be used to highlight a feature such as the eyes, and then force the remainder of the image into an intentionally unfocused background.

No strobe: peacock flounder
[Panasonic GF1 with 45mm lens INON housing, f2.8 at 1/400s, ISO 100]

Summary

Adaptations in this chapter are presented for the novice and expert underwater photographer alike. For every challenge or compromise, there are a wealth of opportunities to balance this. As your freediving image portfolio grows, you will reap the rewards of these opportunities.

- Depth is a determining factor with lens choice, although adaptations exist.
- Shallow water has more opportunities for freedivers than scuba divers.
- Some macro images are possible in ambient light.

With the correct breath-hold, capturing silhouettes is achievable
[Panasonic GF1 with 7–14mm lens, INON housing, f20 at 1/400s, ISO 200]

Lungcraft

> '... and if you gaze for long into an abyss, the abyss gazes also into you'
>
> *Frederick Nietzsche*[1]

Pre-Apneatic Breathing

If there is one factor that will influence the duration of your breath-hold more than any other, it is the way you breathe before you submerge.

Breathing is everything. Yet for most of us we breathe lazily and inefficiently. Some people have to be more efficient with their breathing — small children for instance. The lungs of infants younger than six months have to work harder, so they do things slightly differently. If you happen to have one of these little people to hand, take a moment to watch how their tiny tummies move as they breathe. It is called diaphragmatic breathing, and the technique is very straightforward.

By pushing out your belly as you breathe in, the diaphragm (i.e. large muscle separating the lungs and heart from the abdominal cavity) moves downward and makes more space for the lungs to draw in air. If this feels strange or uncomfortable, it is because unless exercising we have a tendency to shallow-breathe. This is where only a minimal amount of air is drawn in, and the same out. This tends to be sufficient when sedentary in order to exchange the aerobic gases that we absorb/eliminate. This isn't so good for breath-holding though, because shallow breathing leaves 'dead space' in the lungs where carbon dioxide levels are high and oxygen low.

By using diaphragmatic breathing instead we do two things: improve the exchange of gases between air in the lungs and haemoglobin in the blood, and maintain a supply of refreshed air in the lung spaces.

Diaphragmatic breathing needs to be combined with a regulated breathing pattern to make it even more effective for the apneist. By this we mean breathe slowly and deeply — approaching ten seconds for inhalation, and fifteen for exhalation.

---

1   Aphorism 146, in *Beyond Good and Evil* (1886).

Diaphragmatic Breathing Exercise

If you have a moment or two, try this exercise:

1. Sit or lie down and loosen any tight clothing.
2. Put one hand on your chest and the other on your stomach.

Lungs deflated

3. Breathe in slowly and steadily.
4. As you breathe in, push out your stomach and feel it expanding with your hand.

Diaphragm flexed and lower lung lobes inflated

5. Carry on breathing in and feel your other hand move as your chest takes over.

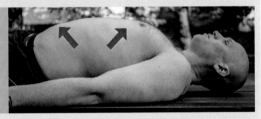

Lungs fully inflated

6. Slowly breathe out and reverse the two sequences above — let air out of your chest and when it is mostly empty pull your stomach in.

Congratulations! You have now mastered diaphragmatic breathing. Not so difficult, is it?

Now try doing this for a few minutes with your eyes closed. When you have finished, do you feel differently to when you started? You should feel more relaxed, perhaps even a little elated. This regulated breathing is taking things a step further, and helps slow down your heart rate. It also reduces carbon dioxide levels in the blood plasma in a controlled manner. Not all breathing preparations are as controlled, and some of the alternatives carry more risk. Take hyperventilation for example.

Contrary to popular belief, **the wrong way to breathe before freediving is by hyperventilating**. This is a rapid and somewhat shallow type of breathing, which takes a certain amount of effort to perform. It causes carbon dioxide levels in the blood to plummet. When you consider that rising carbon dioxide levels are the trigger for us wanting to breathe (rather than low oxygen), then it stands to reason that less carbon dioxide translates into a longer breath-hold. However, it is only the urge to breathe that is elongated, not the physiological need to acquire more oxygen. This physiological need can eventually override the mental control, and that is when hypoxic events commence. Initially cyanosis will appear (a blue tinge in the lips and skin), which then progresses onto loss of motor control (uncontrolled movement in the limbs), followed by loss of consciousness. So with hyperventilation we close the gap between feeling that it is time to breathe and the potential to black out. Obviously not something we want to happen, especially underwater.

Unfortunately another factor makes this worse. Low carbon dioxide levels also cause vasoconstriction to the veins and arteries supplying the brain. In other words the vessels contract and reduce the blood flow. Shallow water blackout (a topic covered in *Chapter 10: Safety*) is a risk in its own right and caused by other factors, so we really don't want to exacerbate that by losing awareness of when breathing becomes a vital necessity.

Previously I mentioned that diaphragmatic breathing reduces carbon dioxide levels, so won't the same effect arise? In fact there will be a closing of this gap of *critical consciousness*, but far less pronounced than from the effects of hyperventilation.

Why would anyone hyperventilate then, or think it was worthwhile? The simplistic view is that it translates into a longer breath-hold due to the lowering of blood carbon dioxide levels. But we now know there is a price to pay for this.

The following series of charts are an indication of how breath-hold preparation can vary the outcome of the breath-hold. They are not related to any one individual, and the terms used are not necessarily common in freediving science or physiology. So where we refer to a Critical Hypoxia Risk percentage, all this means is the difference at zero between the onset of hypoxic signs (such as cyanosis mentioned previously) and at one hundred percent a significant hypoxic event — typically the onset of losing consciousness. The urge to breathe is again expressed as a percentage, with one hundred percent being the point where you'd feel it absolutely necessary to resume breathing.

The statistics are not a literal interpretation — there are far too many variables that would change the values for different divers and individual physiology. What we would expect though, is for the relative changes between each chart to be similar. So where the red area starts to encroach on the green, and the slope of the green decreases, these are the proportional changes anticipated for the majority of individuals.

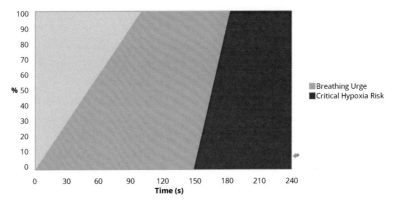

Chart 1: Normal Breathing

With a normal breathing pattern, albeit possibly shallow, we can see that this person is still able to breath-hold for a better than average period. But they do have an urge to resume breathing well before any hypoxia signs or symptoms are present.

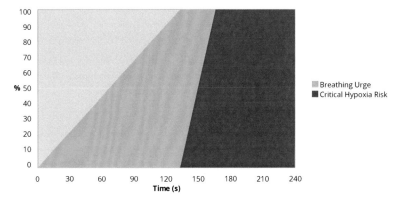

Chart 2: Deep Breathing

Deep breathing has two clear effects — firstly, the urge to resume breathing slows to a longer duration. Secondly, the onset of hypoxia happens earlier, due to partially increased vasoconstriction. We still have a fair gap between the two one hundred percent points. We should not be unduly concerned, but also not complacent about the changing states.

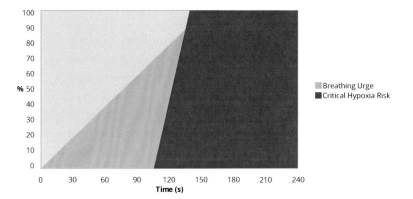

Chart 3: Hyperventilation

In this example hyperventilation brings the onset of hypoxia forward in the timeline, and at the same time elongates the urge to breathe. Something significant happens here — there is a crossover point. Although we don't see the point where the urge to breathe has hit one hundred percent, we know for certain it is after the critical hypoxia risk factor has reached that stage. In other words, some form of hypoxic episode could be expected before the diver feels it absolutely necessary to resume breathing. Although this is an extreme example, as mentioned previously the change in pattern approximates to what actually happens.

We can't say that someone who hyperventilates strongly will end up blacking out any more than we would say that someone who breathes slowly and deeply will not. But there are risks to be considered here and hyperventilation is an increasing risk factor, not a decreasing one.

Breathing In-Water

The principles of pre-apneatic breathing can apply both in the water and out. Many freedivers practice breath-holding in the comfort of their living rooms, and the techniques are near enough the same for both. We do need some equipment to help us in open water though. The very action of breathing makes changes to our buoyancy, and coupled with wave action may mean that our mouths end up being submerged just when we want to breathe in. Snorkels and/or floats are useful utilities here and are discussed in *Chapter 1: Freediving Equipment for Underwater Photography*. A fixed guide line is another aid. You should make use of at least one of these before the dive, as the increased volume of air shifting to and from your lungs will make significant differences to the proportion of your body submerged. Treading water, where you move your arms and legs to keep afloat, is not recommended. It raises metabolism and wastes energy.

How long should you do your preparatory breathing for? Freedivers call this 'breathing-up' and two minutes would normally be considered a minimum. But of course as photographers, we rarely have the luxury of being able to plan ahead like this. Sometimes the action is upon us there and then. This is why using the correct equipment is so important, as items such as fins and wetsuits become a compensating mechanism for extending the dive duration. However, if you are waiting for a pod of dolphins to sweep your way, you may as well be as prepared as possible and have started breathing-up.

The Final Breath

Typically, our final inhalation before submerging should be a deep one, although in *Chapter 8: Neutral Buoyancy* we will find circumstances where this might

Glass and Water

not be the case. For now though, let us assume we want one hundred percent of our lungs filled with fresh air.

In some cases you may want to dive to a deeper level — to photograph a wreck or something interesting on the seabed. In these situations your ears will benefit from a good lungful of air. As you descend deeper, the increase in pressure forces the lung air to reduce in volume, until the point where it is no longer possible to move air down into your mouth (bearing in mind you are usually inverted whilst descending). Without air in the mouth the ears can no longer be equalised and descending further will cause damage to the eardrums. It has to be said though, that diving to these depths — likely to be beyond twenty metres — is certainly not something to be attempted without building up confidence with incremental increases through training. It also leaves little time for composing an image, and only a few freediving underwater photographers are likely to want to venture to these sorts of depths. *Chapter 10: Safety* looks further into risks associated with deep diving. It needs careful consideration and planning, not to mention a partner who is trained and able to perform rescue procedures.

Some subjects prefer to remain at depth, such as the thresher shark. Freediving photography at these depths requires training and preparation. It won't be suitable for everyone.
[Panasonic GF1 with 7–14mm lens, INON housing, f4.0 at 1/80s, ISO 1600]

The Mammalian Dive Reflex

There is an automatic physiological mechanism that marine mammals experience during their periods underwater. Humans have this too, although to a lesser extent. There are three distinct phases: *bradycardia*, *peripheral vasoconstriction* and the *blood shift*. The reflex assists with extending the duration of each dive, and is triggered when receptors in the face come into contact with cold water.

Bradycardia is a slowing down of the heart rate. In humans, the reduction ranges between ten and twenty-five percent. In marine mammals it is a significantly higher percentage. This reduction lessons the release of oxygen to non-essential tissues, preserving it for use by more critical and central organs.

Peripheral Vasoconstriction is a narrowing of capillaries that causes blood circulation to the extremities to be reduced. This enhances the effect of bradycardia, and means that more blood volume is available for use by the heart and brain. (This produces a different effect to vasoconstriction mentioned earlier in relation to hyperventilation, which is caused by low carbon dioxide levels and affects a wider range of blood vessels.)

The *blood shift* is the final phase of the mammalian dive reflex, and relates to the redistribution of blood from the first two phases. Extra blood within the torso is sent to blood vessels in the lungs, which in turn cause the lung alveoli to shrink. This helps prevent lung collapse as a result of the increased ambient water pressure. There is also a lowering of blood pressure.

These adaptations are of benefit to the freediver, as they improve the body's ability to cope with the effects of being underwater at depth.

Technique

In order to take a good deep breath, you will need to exhale, pause, exhale a bit more, pause again, and then push just a little more out. This won't feel comfortable or natural, but it is only for a few seconds. Next you need to breathe in while bearing down on your diaphragm, pushing your stomach outward (as detailed earlier). Once the lower lobes of your lungs are filled, then you can expand your chest and fill the upper half. Don't rush this movement otherwise you won't take in a good fill!

Some freedivers find that if they overfill their lungs, as they crease their torso for the duck-dive, some air finds its way into the stomach. This is nothing to worry about.

The Breath Hold

There are many factors that will determine how long you can hold your breath — hydrodynamics, style and efficiency of kick, buoyancy, etc. We shall look at each of these as we continue through the book.

As your dive progresses, your body will undergo various changes that relate to your period of apnea. Any fullness in the chest will dissipate once you have reached a depth of two or three metres and the water pressure reduces the air volume. At this stage there should be no sensation of needing to breathe, and the feeling should be quite pleasant and relaxed. Of course you may be filming or photographing something quite exciting, and this may have an overriding effect!

There comes the inevitable point where you want to breathe. The most sensible policy is to surface and do just that. But your subject may be just coming into focus, so should you resist the urge and stay longer? My advice would have to be 'no'. It is all too easy for concentration to go into the task at hand and ignore the important signals the body is sending. Also, hypoxia can impair judgment and that shouldn't be overlooked. What to expect though if you do find yourself ten metres down and knowing you have overridden the signals?

Firstly, don't panic! You may well experience 'contractions', which is where part of the brain tries to force a breath by contracting the diaphragm. This is not dissimilar to a hiccough. It is not particularly pleasant, but not catastrophic. Experienced competitive freedivers will often go through several repetitions of these during a dive, although I wouldn't recommend newcomers try such feats of endurance. Just don't let it rattle you. Do the sensible thing — surface.

A relaxed approach to the surface, where a breath of fresh air awaits.
[Panasonic GF1 with 7–14mm lens, INON housing, f8.0 at 1/200s, ISO 400]

Breathing and Breath-Holding Exercises

Yoga

Sometimes my students ask me which are the best exercises for improving their breath-hold. For a long time I have been able to answer with a single word — yoga. Let's break down some of the essentials — the first being chest flexibility. The more flexible your chest, the more efficiently you will be able to

draw in air. Yoga can make improvements here by increasing elasticity/flexibility, improving muscle strength, mind focus, balance and co-ordination. Being able to relax, and to do so fairly quickly is another benefit.

Pre-dive stretch routines are a sensible way to avoid injury, and allow muscles to perform more efficiently. A number of yoga stretches are good for this, although I wouldn't be too prescriptive here, as different positions and movements may suit one person and not the other. Stretches of the leg muscles, feet, chest and neck are all sensible areas to focus on. Starting with the feet and ending with the neck will provide some structure to your chosen routine.

© Sheila Wisdom/yogawisdom.co.uk

Last but not least, yoga appears to have a positive effect on the body's ability to produce myoglobin. This is a muscle-based protein similar to haemoglobin that effectively acts as a reserve supply of oxygen directly for the muscles.

I have never heard anyone tell me that yoga has had a detrimental effect on their freediving, but certainly many have seen improvements. Virtually all world record setting freedivers are advanced practitioners of yoga, and in at least one case an instructor.

Dry Static Apnea

One fairly obvious exercise for making improvements with breath-holding is … breath-holding. This can be carried out in the comfort of your living room or bedroom, and this is referred to as 'dry static apnea'. A fairly straightforward regime would be three repetitions, where the first hold represents seventy-five percent of your effort, the second eighty-five percent, and the final effort ninety to ninety-five percent. Each breath-hold should be separated by two minutes or the duration of the previous hold, whichever is the greater. The main safety consideration is just making sure you aren't in a position to injure yourself in the unlikely circumstance of losing consciousness. If this were to happen, then providing you have no underlying medical condition to cause complications, you would soon regain your consciousness without needing assistance. This shouldn't happen in the first place if your maximum hold doesn't exceed ninety-five percent effort, and you don't hyperventilate. **Static breath-holding in a bath of water is not safe**, and most definitely to be avoided.

One session of static apnea a day is sufficient. If you are doing this over consecutive days, then at least one day's rest after three training days would be sensible. Breath-holding generates free radicals in the body, so a good countermeasure to this is to take antioxidant supplements or plenty of food/drink containing natural antioxidants. Leafy greens, fresh fruit, red peppers and dark berries are all beneficial. Rest is extremely important. It is not just a case of doing this for general well-being, but to aid the whole improvement cycle. I normally avoid any breath-holding for at least twenty-four hours before doing any demanding freediving, and have always found this to be beneficial.

Clubs/Training

One of the most enjoyable ways of conditioning for improved breath-holding, is to train alongside others within a freediving club or group. If you are miles away from the coast or open water this shouldn't present a problem, as many clubs and groups train at swimming pools. AIDA International (the Worldwide Federation for breath-hold diving) has a list of regions that are assembly members, and from here the representative for each country can be found. In the UK this is the British Freediving Association (BFA). The BFA website lists the various freediving clubs and groups up and down the country.[2] Most clubs expect you to provide your own equipment, and not all are commercial enterprises. What they will provide is a supportive environment where you are encouraged to train safely, can typically undertake training courses, and pick up interesting tips and techniques from like-minded freedivers.

There are many other activities and exercises that can help improve breath-holding performance, but the above are good starting points. It is worth taking time to make these preparations, as you'll have the edge when you are on an

2   See http://www.britishfreediving.org/

Technique

important field trip and the extra time afforded by a well-executed breath-hold dive could well make the difference between a good image and a superb one.

Summary

- Deep, diaphragmatic breathing will improve the duration of a breath-hold.
- Hyperventilation should be avoided for the sake of safety.
- A snorkel and/or float is essential in open water.
- The final breath before submerging should be slow and deep.
- If your body demands breathing, then listen and surface, do not fight the urge.
- For many, yoga is beneficial for overall conditioning.
- A freediving club provides the right environment and expertise for training.

Technique

6

Ultimate master of the fin kick:
Atlantic spotted dolphin
© Laura Storm/Planet Plankton
[Canon EOS 550D with 15mm
lens, SEA&SEA housing,
f7.1 at 1/640s, ISO 200]

Finning

'Today I almost feel as if I am naked if I don't have a camera with me under-water. It has become a part of me, just like my long-bladed carbon fins'

Fred Buyle[1]

The Priority Technique

I am frequently told by would-be freediving photographers, 'I need to improve my breath-hold so that I can stay under for longer'. Unfortunately, this is not where the best gains are to be made. Improving underwater finning technique surpasses breath-hold improvement … with ease. Some of competitive free-diving's best athletes have only slightly better-than-average breath-holds, and yet set impressive distance or depth records. This is simply down to exemplary finning style and technique. This chapter is a short introduction to finning. Further detail and insights can be found in *Chapter 9: Hydrodynamics*.

Fin Type

As covered in *Chapter 1: Freediving Equipment for Underwater Photography* there are two main divisions of fins — the monofin and the bifin. The single-bladed monofin is primarily geared to the domain of the competitive freediver. For underwater photographers its power advantages are outweighed by its lack of manoeuvrability, so we'll not be exploring that option here. If you have a specific interest in learning how to use one, you would ideally need some expert coaching and several weeks or even months of training to master its use.

The mere existence of the monofin means that what scuba divers generally refer to as 'fins' we must redefine as bifins or stereo fins. I'll excuse the unen-lightened for calling them flippers.

---

1   *Apnea* (2011) Perpignan: Catapac.

Monofin: supreme propulsion tool ... but not for the underwater photographer

Style Variation

There are a number of finning techniques that could be considered for forward motion, although to my mind only one is a clear choice for the underwater photographer.

Firstly there is the dolphin kick, where the legs move in unison as one entity. This kick is a definite requirement for the monofinner, but many freedivers also make use of this with bifins. When executed correctly it can be quite relaxing, have a graceful appearance and be efficient ... but not when carrying a camera rig. This is because the whole body needs to undulate with the arms free of cumbersome objects such as cameras.

A finning technique you would be unlikely to find freedivers using is the modified frog kick used by cave and wreck scuba divers. This is a kick where the legs are angled at ninety degrees in order to keep the foot level above the hips. It stops bottom sediment from being churned up and reducing visibility. Whilst it is feasible you might want to freedive and take photographs in an overhead environment, there is a lot more to consider than just finning technique, and therefore a speciality training course offered by a freediving instructor with the relevant experience would be more appropriate. Any forwards motion that is powered by the frog kick needs to have a good reason or other benefit. This is because when using this kick with fins, there is a counterproductive drag factor to take into account. On the other hand, if you find yourself in a situation without fins, then a well-executed frog kick tends to be more efficient than the 'flutter' kick.

The final and most sensible finning technique for the freediving photographer, is the flutter kick. If you are a scuba diver then you are likely to know it already. It is the alternate up-and-down movement of each leg that forces your fins to push against water resistance and drive your body forward.

Analysis of the Flutter Kick

There are three pivot points in each leg where the majority of movement occurs. These are the hip joint, knee and ankle. On any given fin stroke each point needs to pivot in the same direction at the same time, and by roughly the same amount — approximately twenty degrees per joint.

Measuring individual joint movement is not really the best way to analyse this; it makes more sense to address the full waist to toe view. A classic mistake is to make too much movement at the knee joint. When this happens you will look as if you are riding an imaginary underwater bicycle. Conversely, too much movement in the hip and too little in the knee will produce a stiff looking stroke which will rock the pelvis.

Flutter kick © Fred Buyle/nektos.net

Pivoting all three points in unison enables a fluid movement that uses all the lower muscle groups and tendons. This will provide more power and produce less fatigue than overuse of one or two.

The amplitude of your stroke is the measurement between the highest and lowest points that your legs reach during a fin cycle. This needs to be approximately fifty to sixty percent of the maximum extent possible. Although a full, wide kick may feel quite powerful, it also acts as a partial brake against the oncoming flow of water.

In regard to the frequency of the kick, again less is more. Too much and your oxygen consumption will increase. You can of course fin too slowly and end up losing speed and momentum. Fin kick amplitude and frequency are examined in more detail in *Chapter 9: Hydrodynamics*.

Result of too much knee rotation: drag

Common Issues

One issue to consider is fin slippage. As each leg starts its downward or upward stroke, the counterforce of the water will seek the path of least resistance. It can lead the freediver to subconsciously make a slight twist to the ankle, and hence the fin slices through the water at an angle. This loses valuable power. It is not exclusively a technique issue. Most freediving bifins have side rails designed to minimise fin slippage, but some are minimal or absent altogether. For these types of fin, the user will need good foot/ankle control. Alternatively you could fit side rails yourself, but buying fins where they have been included in the design would be preferable.

As each leg meets at the mid-point there will be times when one fin makes contact with the other. It happens from time-to-time, even with the most accomplished freediver. Fins are designed to resist damage from this, but it doesn't make for efficient movement if the contact is on every stroke. I don't advocate correcting this to the extent that it would never happen, otherwise

Glass and Water

the chances are that the legs are then too far apart and creating side drag. As with many technique corrections it is a case of evaluating, making minor adjustments and then monitoring. With practice each fin will brush by the other with just a few millimetres to spare, and you'll have an intuitive awareness of this. In technical terms this is known as proprioception or proprioceptive adaptation — which is the unconscious perception of movement and spatial orientation arising from stimuli within the body itself. There's a name for everything!

Although not something that directly reduces efficiency, a rubbing foot pocket can be quite uncomfortable and cause blistering. Neoprene socks eliminate this, and should be worn as a matter of course on each dive. If the cause of the rubbing is an oversized foot pocket, this definitely will reduce efficiency. A tight-fitting pocket means that more energy is transferred into the fin structure.

Side rails (Let's not twist again)

Alternate Adaptations

Pacing

Very often you will dive beneath the surface and have a specific target or location you want to reach. Sometimes not — it may be that your subjects are all around you, or yet to be located and you are simply out there exploring. It could also be that you only have a short distance to swim in order to reach your target. In these situations, then a slower pace will pay dividends. By slowing down your movement, your oxygen consumption/carbon dioxide production decreases. What will increase as a result of controlled, slower movement is your breath-hold duration. In these circumstances, a modified kick can be used. By reducing movement at the knee and hip, but keeping the ankle movement about the same as normal, then the larger muscle groups use less fuel and oxygen. This again makes an improvement to the breath-hold. Everything is under your control here — you are able to choose between speed and duration, depending on your requirements at the time.

Kick/Kick/Glide

A slightly more advanced finning technique is to simply take a break. Well, at least for every third fin kick. With this non-kick you just take a rest and use your momentum to glide. Your first reaction to this might be, 'What a brilliant idea — three for the price of two!', but don't forget that you will still decelerate on your glide, and have to counter this with acceleration on the first of the two kicks. Also, you need to make sure that your legs are together and perfectly in-line with your body on the glide. This is why this technique is considered advanced — get the positioning or kick force wrong and you may be no better off. It is something to practice, experiment with and make comparisons. This is known in freediving circles as the 'kick/kick/glide' technique.

Sometimes the less-is-more philosophy has to go out of the window. You may have to fight against current, or apply a bit more speed to avoid some hazard. There are also freediving's ups and downs to consider. Descending from the surface always requires more force, as does ascending from a deep dive. In both cases this relates to buoyancy, which you can read more about in *Chapter 8: Neutral Buoyancy*.

Cramping Your Style

Clearly, bad finning technique will cause you to slow down, shorten the duration of your dive, or both. A far worse situation though, is leg cramp. This is not an uncommon condition, especially with the novice freediver. As mentioned in *Chapter 1: Freediving Equipment for Underwater Photography*, fins are available in a variety of stiffness grades, and the stiffer the blade the more force is needed to drive it. A fin that is too stiff can cause muscle cramp. A tall, muscular individual may be able to cope with a stiff grade fin, but those of a leaner or slighter build should be looking at the softer variety.

Cramp can be released by stretching the affected muscle. This can be achieved by gripping the fin tip and pulling the fin towards you at the same time as straightening out the affected leg. When at the surface, having a snorkel in your mouth is helpful as you may tend to roll forward. If you need your partner's assistance, don't be afraid to ask. I advise releasing a cramp at the surface rather than attempting this underwater.

Relieving cramp

We have covered the basics on how to flutter kick, variations in propulsion, and a few of the common issues. Some more advanced details can be found in *Chapter 9: Hydrodynamics*.

Summary

- Choose an appropriate pair of fins.
- Focus attention on the flutter kick.
- Synchronise leg joint movements and rotate by a similar amount.
- Don't make too deep a fin kick.
- 'Kick back' with your speed and don't rush.
- Be aware of fin slippage and fin contact.
- Practice/try out other techniques, such as 'dead slow' and 'kick/kick/glide'.
- Use extra force for ascents, descents, current and hazard avoidance.
- Avoiding frequent leg cramp may mean using fins with less stiff blades.

7

Turtle down
[Panasonic GF1 with 7–14mm lens,
INON housing, f10 at 1/125s, ISO 100]

Descents and Ascents

'From birth, man carries the weight of gravity on his shoulders. He is bolted to earth. But man has only to sink beneath the surface and he is free'

Jaques Yves Cousteau[1]

This chapter deals with the ups and downs of freediving. The descent can be one of the most daunting prospects, and is likely to pose more of a challenge to most people than the return journey to the surface. This is especially true for the underwater photographer, who has additional equipment to descend with. Struggling with buoyancy, ear problems and disorientation are all common problems. The good news though, is that there are also common solutions.

Descents

As with advice you will find echoed throughout this book, the key to good technique is training (through instruction) and practice (with someone monitoring). For this reason, the advice here will consist of key hints and tips to help you on your way. With descents, a blow-by-blow account of every detail would be overwhelming, and something you are better placed to learn through training.

An aid that helps a lot with descents is a vertical guide line, attached to a float. It allows you to follow the most direct route downwards without having to crane your neck back to see where the bottom is. This in turn means that photographic equipment can be held below your head without obscuring your view.

Warming Up

This step is important, as it helps with the duration of subsequent dives, which is key to the objectives of the underwater photographer. It should be considered part of your dive routine unless your subject is fast approaching and time does not allow. The warm up should simply consist of a relaxed dive to your neutrally buoyant point. This is then followed by a pause for a time period that doesn't

1   *Time* (28 March 1960).

Technique

leave you with a challenging breath-hold struggle, and a relaxed float up to the surface. The method of descent for this would ideally be an arm-by-arm pull-down on a guide line. However, if you have no guide line or insufficient weight on the end of it, this may not be possible and you'll need to fin ... gently. The idea is to condition your physiology to both the effects of pressure and carbon dioxide build-up but without expending too much effort. In turn this will improve your comfort and performance on the next dive.

Regarding other pre-dive preparations, a gentle pre-dive stretch of the neck (as if you were trying to touch one ear on to your shoulder) can be beneficial, as it can improve ear equalisation. Also, as you descend, keep your chin tucked into your chest. As with the previous neck exercise, this has a stretching effect on the Eustachian tube, allowing an easier passage of air through it.

Float, flag and weighted guide line

Duck Dive

In order to become submerged, the most efficient method is the 'duck dive'. The objective here is to use the weight of your legs to push the rest of you under the water, or at least as far as possible. Bend downward at the waist and then swing the legs upwards to realign with your body. You will begin sinking.

Probably the first moment you will be wishing you had a third arm will be half way through this manoeuvre. Assuming one hand is carrying your photographic equipment, then you only have one left to make the initial arm stroke. This stroke is necessary to propel your legs and fins beneath the surface. You certainly should not start kicking until they are, otherwise valuable oxygen is consumed for virtually no propulsion. You may then find that you are at odds with equalisation, as you will probably be deep enough for water pressure to be building up before your free hand is able to reach your nose. Pre-equalisation at the surface can counteract this. Don't be tempted to try using nose clips on the outside of your mask. This will prevent the inner mask space from being equalised, and will result in mask squeeze characterised by deep red lines on the face and bloodshot eyes.

As underwater photographers we already have enough to think about, so we should try to learn our descent tasks so that they become automatic. The key things we should be doing, in order, are as follows:

- Slight pre-equalisation of ears at surface.
- Slow, deep preparatory breath.
- Snorkel placed in float / with partner.
- Concentration on duck dive, with no leg kicks until fin tips fully submerged.
- Ear equalisation with hand left in-place.
- Chin and elbow both tucked in.
- Powerful leg thrusts for first few metres.
- If using a descent line, ensure you are parallel to it.
- Continual or frequent equalisation of ears and mask.
- Reduce power to fin kicks as depth increases.
- Listen for dive computer alarm to alert you to a target depth.
- Resist temptation to look downward until you are near your target depth.

SOUPA Camera Deployment

There is a camera deployment strategy you can consider in order to simplify your descent, but it comes with risk. If you have a float with a weighted guide line attached, then a tube or some other stop can be attached at whatever depth you decide. You can then clip your camera to the line with a couple of karabiners and let go. As long as you don't have camera equipment that floats, and the karabiners' internal diameters are not wider than the tube's external diameter, then it will sink to the prescribed depth and stop at the tube top. You are then able to execute the perfect dive to where your camera is, unclip it and away you go. I appreciate that to many a reader this may sound like an accident waiting to happen. Every attachment would need to be checked and double-checked, with redundancy built-in, by which I mean the connection of more than one clip and lanyard, so that the failure of one doesn't result in detachment from the guide line. Watching your full-frame SLR disappear into the blue could easily be a painful experience otherwise.

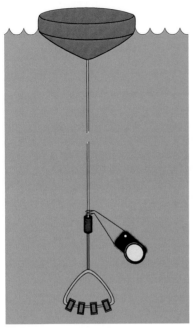

SOUPA

For want of a better term, I refer to this as a Submersible Optics Underwater Platform Assembly or 'SOUPA'. It isn't going to appeal to everyone, and there will only be certain situations where it is useful. This is likely to be beyond a depth of five metres, where the subject is either static or predictable, and you need to spend some time on the photography for example macro. I'm offering this as an option to consider rather than a firm recommendation, and if your camera detaches from your SOUPA I'm afraid that will be your own responsibility!

The tube used to stop the deployed camera rig should have no sharp edges, and the guide line should pass through the middle then be looped up and back through the middle a second time. At the exit point it can be knotted to the bottom loop so that the tube stays put.

On the subject of knots, if there was only one knot that I was prepared to learn it would be the figure-eight knot. It is shown here attaching the guide line to the underside of the float.

I won't go into the tying techniques as these are better demonstrated (there are clips on YouTube), but they are fairly straightforward. I use this knot at both ends of the guide line. The bight (or loop) at the bottom end, I thread a weight belt through, with added clip on the loose end of the belt so that

Figure-eight knot

Glass and Water

it can't detach if the belt buckle comes undone. You can also use this knot to tie off your stop tube as mentioned previously.

One extra precaution (and part of the reason to have a separate stop in the first place) is to have the tube high enough on the line so that your rig doesn't come into contact with the lead weights at the very bottom.

Camera Positioning

Assuming then that your camera equipment remains in your non-equalising hand, and that you are now fully submerged, you will want to position your rig where it least impedes downward progress. In *Chapter 9: Hydrodynamics* I describe how to do this for horizontal swimming. The approach for a descent is pretty much the same, but the buoyancy of your photographic equipment will have a bearing. Again, in *Chapter 9: Hydrodynamics* you will learn how a

slightly heavier-than-water rig can have a benefit for swimming parallel to the surface, and with descents this too holds true. If your camera is below the level of your head and in-line with your body, then one of your arms will just guide and secure it. It will also help maintain a minimum cross-section of moving mass. If it has positive buoyancy then additionally you have to over-come the housed camera's natural tendency to float. Smaller camera rigs can be held close to your body alongside the hips.

As an interesting aside, competitive freedivers also have this issue of needing several pairs of hands and have come up with a novel solution. The discipline of No-Fins Constant Weight involves descending using modified

Progressing duck dive: the camera moving into the overhead position

breast stroke where two arms are needed, leaving none available to help with equalisation. There are special goggles available — generically called 'liquid goggles' — that have a lens that will allow the human eye to see without an air space present within the focal length. You simply fill them with water. Water being non-compressible this then means the freediver can also attach nose clips, and thereby free up the equalising hand. It is of academic interest only as the modified vision in such goggles is not of sufficient quality for using photographic equipment. At least not at the time of writing, that is.

Practicing your technique at a freediving training session will pay dividends when it comes to descents, even if the deep end of the pool is only three metres. I mentioned earlier about mental checklists due to the rapid succession of tasks to think about. Regular practice will help some of these become second nature. When you have arrived at where you wish to be, all you want to be thinking about is photography rather than, 'Did I just forget to do something on my duck dive?'. This is also an opportunity to point out that it is generally a good idea to have as many of your camera settings as possible set up in advance before you dive. Time underwater while breath-holding is precious and shouldn't be spent waiting for your camera to power on.

Camera Checklist (Digital Stills)

- Check battery and media card for capacity.
- Remove any neoprene port cover or dust caps.
- 'Dip test' the camera housing in the water and look for bubbles escaping.
- Ensure any lanyard used is attached to you and the camera rig.
- Turn camera on.
- Turn strobes on (if using) and make appropriate strobe settings.
- Ensure camera is set to correct flash mode if strobes being used.
- Choose appropriate mode setting.
- Check/set *ISO, f-stop* and *shutter speed*.
- Check/set *focusing method* and *focus area points*.
- Check recording *format, resolution, exposure compensation* and other non-primary settings.
- Pre-set *manual white balance* at the appropriate depth (if using).
- Adjust strobe arms if strobe being used.

Some situations need careful consideration. If you need to dive deep, are shooting wide-angle and using strobe, then most photographers will want the strobe(s) to be sitting on well-extended arms. Having this configured before the dive will not make for an easy descent. There may need to be a compromise in sacrificing some time positioning the arms after the descent. I suspect though for some, it will be a case of dispensing with the strobes for deeper shots. For others scuba will be the solution.

An efficient descent has left enough bottom time for dolphin
photography © Laura Storm/Planet Plankton

Bottom Time

Having reached your target depth, you are either where you want to be to start shooting or you need to swim elsewhere. If you are ready to start shooting then the information in *Chapter 8: Neutral Buoyancy* will be of use, and if you need to swim on then *Chapter 9: Hydrodynamics* will provide some useful advice. The other option you may be faced with is an immediate return to the surface, if you have overcommitted on your depth target for example. This brings us to an important point.

If you master the techniques for freediving descents fairly quickly, you may well discover that your ability to reach significant depth is greater than your physiology can cope with. Specifically, the risk of an hypoxic event. The only way to determine this is by a progressive build-up to greater depths over time, which brings about a gradual adaptation. If there are two freediving principles I simply cannot overstate, they are: **never freedive alone** and **learn techniques correctly on an approved training course**. I also recommend not diving deeper than ten metres unless you are the holder of an advanced freediving qualification.

Surfacing

You should be pleased to learn that returning to the surface is less complicated than the journey down. Probably the biggest contribution to this is that there is no need to equalise the ears — they do this on their own as the air expands. This means both hands are free to hold camera equipment.

If you have dived to a depth beyond your neutrally buoyant state, then some extra leg effort will be required in order to pick up momentum. The effort put into this should be limited and not a maximum amount. Your muscles will be working with reduced oxygen availability, and there will be resistance (to a varying degree) encountered due to your camera rig. To avoid sudden muscle fatigue, it is better to not over-exert any of the major muscle groups. Therefore when you want extra power use only as much as is really needed.

As you progress with your ascent, buoyancy will increase and mean you can reduce your finning effort. In fact when you reach a point where your upward lift feels sufficient, you can cease finning altogether.

As soon as you have surfaced, then breathe out fully and then breathe in. Breathing out below the surface is often a sign of shallow water blackout, so although you may not be experiencing this, a trained freediving partner may think you are in difficulty if you breathe out early. A subsequent and unnecessary rescue will risk damage to, or loss of, camera equipment.

If you have chosen to dive with your snorkel in your mouth (not ideal for both safety and hydrodynamic reasons) then do not be tempted to 'blast clear' the water when you surface (i.e. blowing it out through the top). This wastes energy and the noise may disturb the subject of your pursuit. Sound travels

Glass and Water

further underwater, and a manta ray travelling in your direction may well alter course. Just let the water drain off of its own accord and tip out the remaining few drops.

Your dive partner should be nearby, so give them some indication all is well — the traditional diver's 'ok' signal is recognised globally.

Recovery

Post dive breathing should really be similar to breathing up prior to the dive, which means deeply and pushing down on the diaphragm. Ideally at this point, keeping afloat should involve minimal kicking of the legs. If you have a flotation device then there is no need to do this at all. Alternatively, breathing face down through your snorkel will enable you to float and therefore cease kicking. Leg muscles burn significant quantities of oxygen. Even though you will have started breathing again it takes a certain period of time for haemoglobin to bond to the fresh oxygen molecules. So if you are metabolising this within key muscle groups in the legs, you could be sending a depressed body oxygen percentage even lower. In addition, this will have a bearing on the duration of your next dive should you be planning one.

Technique

Having gulped a few mouthfuls of fresh air, there could be every temptation to dive again immediately, especially if there is something worthwhile to photograph and which might not hang around. It is your call but the expectation can only be that of a very short dive. Ideally a rest period of between five and ten minutes should be considered (depending upon depth and duration of the dive just completed). Beyond ten minutes and your carbon dioxide tolerance will begin to fade.

Recovery, post dive

Ears and Eyes

A clear difference between scuba and freediving is the dive profile. The

Descents and Ascents

87

freediver is likely to have many ascents and descents whereas a scuba diver is likely to have only one of each. Be aware that this can be tiring and frequent equalisations may also stress the ears. If equalisations are becoming painful, then your Eustachian tubes may have become inflamed and will need to be rested.

Be mindful of the effects of hypothermia and dehydration as your diving session progresses. Both have a negative impact on breath-hold performance. A generally observed rule with freediving and getting cold, is that shivering is the sign to finish diving and seek out warmth. It is also easy to become dehydrated through lack of fluid intake, and the effect of moderate activity over a long period.

Last but not least, be generous with your awareness! What do we typically do after taking a series of photographs? Review them on the LCD display, of course. In the meantime the sea could be picking up, your boat slipping into the distance, or a swarm of jellyfish swelling up from the depths. Even worse your diving partner may have descended, with his or her safety net non-existent as you scroll on to the next image.

Glass and Water

Summary

If there's one message that should be clear from this chapter, it is that task loading increases during descents and ascents. Therefore the more techniques become second nature, the more focus can be switched back to photography. To review:

- Consider the benefits of a guide line/float.
- Pre-dive preparations will elongate your time underwater.
- There are various techniques to solve problematic ear equalisations.
- Descent profile needs attention throughout.
- Descents are trickier carrying a camera, but there are coping mechanisms.
- Let your training and experience set your depth.
- Vary finning force on your ascent.
- Be aware of events around you, especially your partner's well-being.

Technique

8

Wildlife videographer Doug Allan (shown filming humpback whales) is notable for being proficient with freediving buoyancy skills. He has it down to a tee, and his other freediving techniques are very good too. He is a good example to follow. © Sue Flood, Tartan Dragon Ltd.

Neutral Buoyancy

'You go down to the bottom of the sea, where the water isn't even blue anymore, where the sky is only a memory, and you float there, in the silence'

Jacques Mayol [1]

Technique

The state of neutral buoyancy is the nirvana scuba divers aim for. Freediving photographers at least make a nod toward achieving this neutrality; not all achieve the right balance.

If you watch modern natural history documentaries, the last ten minutes often show a feature on how some scenes were shot. For underwater films taken by freediving videographers, this can be invaluable viewing. What I sometimes see is a videographer using up valuable energy correcting his or her under-weighting. To the untrained eye it can be easy to miss, but if you look at the body angles relative to the surface, it becomes apparent.

Do freedivers really need to worry about this? Does it matter if we look ungainly on our dives? The answer to both is an emphatic 'yes'. Every fin kick we make should be for the purpose of motion towards a location or target. If it is a corrective kick to offset over or under-weighting, then it is wasted energy that translates into a reduced breath-hold.

Our spatial awareness will also improve considerably when not having to fight the forces trying to take us up or down. Not only does it look right, it feels right.

Analysing Mass

Before we start to put the right practices into place, let's analyse the factors that affect our buoyancy. Firstly, it would be a good idea to compare what we are and what we carry, to the density of water.

The constituent parts we contain or carry that are lighter than water (i.e. that float) are air, neoprene and fat (or more flatteringly, 'bioprene'). Put a

---

1   *The Big Blue* (1988) Directed by Luc Besson. USA: Gaumont.

wetsuit into a bath of water and it will float. Air is contained within our lungs, sinuses and mouth cavity. Some also finds its way into our intestines, alongside other gases such as methane. All of these gases are less dense than water and therefore provide an upward force or lift. The distribution of this lift will vary in proportion to the location of the different substances. We normally have a fair volume of air in our lungs and head, so more lift is applied here and hence we naturally float toward the surface in a heads-up position.

Our bones and muscle tissue are heavier than water. This creates an opposing force to *lift* that we can refer to as *sink*. Everything else quite literally, hangs in the balance. A large form system with heavy accessories will sink, whereas a small form system in a compact housing may well float. Most mask/snorkel/fin combinations will sink, although some lighter construction items may not.

A floating freediver with heavier body parts (his limbs), sinking downward.
Without a wetsuit, the downward angles would be more pronounced.

Taking everything into account, what would we expect to happen if a medium build freediver in a wetsuit (and no weight belt), were to jump into the sea? I'm sure most of us would expect to see him or her float. I certainly would.

However, if we were to observe a lean and muscular freediver wearing no wetsuit, carrying a large form camera, jump into a freshwater lake, we might see something quite different. Especially if he had only taken, say, half a lungful of air. He may not sink like the proverbial stone, but would need some effort to stay at the surface. I'd expect this diver to be negatively buoyant.

A freediving photographer with lean body mass and thin wetsuit
has easily sunk to the bottom of this swimming pool

The Physics of Pressure

Increasing depth will increase pressure, reduce the volume of our gas spaces, and therefore eventually make us sink. We know that certain parts of our bodies and equipment make us float, and that some cause us to sink. We also know that, as we dive deeper, rising water pressure increases the sink force. For the sake of efficiency, we would like to achieve near-neutral buoyancy at a certain depth, but certainly not at the surface. Here we would like to have positive buoyancy for the sake of safety and comfort.

In the majority of cases we are going to find that the forces of lift by far outweigh those of sink, and therefore make: a) our neutral buoyancy point too deep; and b) descending somewhat of a struggle. So we use a very dense material — lead — and typically attach this to a belt around our hips.

If our lake-diving muscle man wanted to balance forces, clearly adding lead would contribute more to his problem. An easy solution here would be for him to wear a wetsuit, which in a cold lake he may well be grateful for anyway! It is probably also worth mentioning at this point that fresh water is less dense than salt water, and therefore less ballast is needed to make us sink in fresh water.

Technique

Left: Freediver who has stopped finning at depth, and is now sinking.
Right: Same diver on the same dive, but at a significantly shallower depth, who is now floating up to the surface without the need to fin.

Finding Your Depth

The next couple of questions you may be asking are 'At what depth should I be neutrally buoyant?' and 'How do I work that out?' To answer the first question, you need to decide at which point in the dive you are likely to be finning in a horizontal position. Wherever this is, then you will want to maximise the efficiency of your kick, and you now know that being almost neutrally buoyant is the key to this.

For the sake of safety, the precise neutral point should be targeted at least two metres deeper than the depth you wish to swim at. If you were to lose consciousness at your swimming depth, then at least you would start to float rather than sink. The loss of efficiency will be minimal, and worth the safety margin.

I'd expect the majority of freediving photographers to *not* want to be neutrally buoyant any deeper than twenty metres, and I'd recommend that five metres be the shallowest depth. Being neutral shallower than five metres will make breathing at the surface a bit of an effort —the extra weight required will lower the body position at the surface, especially on full exhale. With the lungs lower down, water pressure mounts around them. Deeper than twenty metres your time will be too short to get a decent composition, unless you have competitor level breath-holding abilities.

Establishing the neutral point is quite straightforward. A depth gauge or dive computer in freediving mode is needed, as is a weighted rope or line tied off at the surface (an anchor line will make do). A full deep breath should be taken at the surface and then you simply pull or swim down to the depth you want to be neutrally buoyant at, as shown on your depth gauge. When you reach this depth, grab the rope to stop yourself. You should then release your grip and monitor your depth gauge. If the depth increases, then you are negatively buoyant and will need to remove lead from your belt. If it decreases you are positively buoyant and will need to add lead. Adding and removing lead is carried out at the surface, and shouldn't be in more than 1 kg increments. Failing to release the rope often

Establishing neutrality

gives a false sense of depth if there are waves moving the line up and down. Better to trust your gauge.

If you find yourself without a depth gauge or dive computer, then there is an alternative method you can use to determine if you are moving up or down. Focus on the sensation in your ears. If you can feel pressure mounting, then you are certainly sinking. On the other hand, if you can feel a fullness and/or air escaping through your Eustachian tubes, then air is expanding. This means you are floating upward.

If you need to fine-tune things, then you can sacrifice a small amount of lung volume to decrease lift. As long as you have taken a few deep breaths of fresh air, then breathing out, up to no more than an estimated third of this won't have a huge impact on your breath-hold time. What little you lose from this will be more than made up by the efficiency of your finning. Consider that average human lungs typically hold four to five litres of air and that translates into four or five kilograms on the weight belt. So most of us *should* be able to emulate adding up to an extra kilogram of lead by breathing out a little as I previously described. Needless to say, that can be quite useful. One caveat I would add with sacrificing lung air is to avoid doing this on deeper dives.

Using Equipment to Get the Balance Right

Can we assume that piling on lead weight to offset buoyancy of neoprene is sufficient to maximise efficiency of fin kicks when we are neutral? Unfortunately not. The lead weight has mass that takes energy to propel. What we can do though is use an open-cell freediving suit which has much better thermal properties than scuba wetsuits. Personally, I find that a 3mm tailor-made two-piece open-cell suit is perfectly comfortable in water temperatures as low as 20° Celcius. In a 3mm scuba wetsuit, most divers will start to get chilly below 26°, myself included. The end result is that you can use a thinner wetsuit when using an open-cell type, and therefore less lead weight to offset the buoyancy.

Earlier on, I described how camera variations will either sink or float. For those housings that float, these are frequently supplied with a small lead weight to neutralise flotation. I would generally advise that you fit this weight onto the housing, even though this increases the obvious risk of the rig sinking should you inadvertently let go of it. I would also advise against excessive use of the increasingly popular ball-joint float arms with a large form system. Basically, I'd prefer to have a camera rig that is slightly negative, and for good reason.

1a   1b

1a: A diver without a camera, and not moving forward. His body angles upward as the floatation acts from the lung area of his body.
1b: The same diver fins in the direction of the arrow, but now angles in the opposite direction. This is because he is positively buoyant and must counteract the flotation force in order to maintain a constant depth. This is an inefficient profile.

2a   2b

2a: The diver stops finning again and is handed a negatively buoyant camera. This pivots the diver into a neutrally buoyant and horizontal position.
2b: Now when the diver swims forward, his neutral buoyancy means that his profile is parallel to the direction he is swimming in, and efficiency is maximised.

If the top half of our body is more buoyant than the lower, then strapping weight around our waist doesn't bring us into a nice hydrodynamically efficient horizontal position. We could take a leaf out of the books of competitive freediving and use a neck weight, but these can be a little impractical for other reasons (such as using up valuable baggage allowance when flying). A negatively buoyant camera rig (as long as it is only 1–2 kg negatively buoyant) is the perfect solution. When carried in the shoulder region or in front of the head, the mass will help pivot our bodies into a horizontal position. Just be mindful to not let go of the housing, or you can connect it to a Velcro wrist strap via a lanyard.

The suggestion to not use floating ball-joint arms may not sit well with some readers, especially those who have either invested in them or who have been advised to the contrary. Heavily weighted camera systems put strain on the wrists, and cause destabilisation that can in-turn increase camera shake.

The benefit of a slightly overweighted system only really exists on the occasions where you are likely to need to swim horizontally underwater. Also, you may have a particularly heavy configuration that exceeds the 1–2 kg sink force I suggested. Floating strobe arms may therefore be necessary in certain cases. As with all the points covered in this book, other good techniques or equipment modifications still help to offset the compromises.

Through experimenting with your buoyancy — something which I thoroughly recommend you do — then you may find that for reaching your desired neutrality at optimum depth, you are less buoyant at the surface than you'd like to be. Certainly less so than the average snorkeller. This is where a float can be put to good use, and/or a snorkel.

Honeycomb cowfish — neutral spatiality © Laura Storm/ Planet Plankton
[Canon EOS 550D with 60mm lens, SEA&SEA housing, f13 at 1/80s, ISO 100]

Glass and Water

Summary

As soon as you start swimming underwater in a more neutrally buoyant state, you'll realise the benefits. Your confidence will increase and you will be able to concentrate more on your photography.

- Swimming when neutrally buoyant is more efficient and improves spatial awareness.
- Typically there are more factors that make us float rather than sink.
- The deeper we go, the more we sink.
- The saltier the water, the more we float.
- Don't make a neutral point any shallower than five metres.
- A small amount of lung air can be sacrificed to produce a little extra negative buoyancy, if needed.
- Custom made freediving wetsuits enable thinner composition, and in turn less ballast.
- Some camera weight can mean better distribution for correct profile.
- Snorkel and/or float use should be considered mandatory when optimising buoyancy.
- For the sake of safety, swim with some positive buoyancy.

Technique

9

Squid squad — backward movers but shaped for it
[Panasonic GF1 with 7–14mm lens, INON
housing, f9 at 1/100s, ISO 200]

Hydrodynamics

'The dolphin's ability to reach and exceed a speed of 30 knots is due to their hydrodynamic contours and characteristics of the skin that eliminate the turbulence caused by the movement of any immersed body'

Jacques Mayol[1]

Being hydrodynamic is like being aerodynamic, except underwater. Submarines are designed to be hydrodynamic, but we unfortunately are not.

Water is eight-hundred times denser than air. Car manufacturers seek improved performance in the design of their cars by maximising aerodynamic efficiency, so any savings we can make underwater will be proportionally better. Nature has seen fit to sculpt its swimming occupants in a shape that allows water to move around, not against — just about any non-bottom-dwelling fish would be a good example.

One or two of my freediving associates believe themselves to be descended from dolphins, although I do question that particular evolutionary diversion. If we were, then what a shame we lost that sleek profile and breath-holding ability! We can however, look at aquatic mammals and, by comparison, see what attributes we need to adopt in order to improve our efficiency.

Physiology

Let's start by looking at our anatomy and outer layers. What springs to mind as your outermost layer? Most people immediately think of their skin. Intrinsically linked and more specifically, it is your hair. It is useful insulation for keeping us warm out of the water, but when submerged it only serves to slow us down. More than you would imagine. The easy solution to this is to cover up with a wetsuit. More specifically a wetsuit with a hood, so that as much body and head hair are contained as possible. Even if the hair on your head may be a

---

1   *Homo Delphinus: The Dolphin Within Man* (7th Edn., 2000) Florida: Idelson-Gnocchi Ltd. Publishing.

distant memory an integrated hood ensures the flow of water goes around your shoulders, not into the suit.

Mankind seeks to engineer aerodynamic efficiency;
dolphins have evolved the hydrodynamic equivalent

What of skin itself? Well, underneath there is a layer of subcutaneous fat. As you accelerate and decelerate, something rather interesting happens that you may not be aware of. The layer of fat and soft connective tissue produces a rippling effect. This will vary according to age, fitness, body mass index etc., but you may be unpleasantly surprised if someone filmed you swimming and then showed you the playback slowed down. Most people are subject to this to some extent, but the significant point here is that corrugated skin adds drag. To solve this, simply apply the previous solution by squeezing yourself into a wetsuit.

A decent tailor-made freediving wetsuit will apply light pressure all over and keep any embarrassing rippling at bay. It is well worth considering a suit with a 'smooth skin' outer layer as well. Water molecules experience less friction with these.

With skin and hair covered (quite literally), there can't really be much else to improve on with our profile, can there? In some cases there can. Carrying extra weight around your midriff (and I'm not referring to the lead variety here) is another point of resistance. Layers of soft connective tissue, muscle and subcutaneous fat all contribute to drag. Diet and exercise play an important part in the sculpting process, and normalising body fat percentage can only help with streamlining.

Natural Hydrodynamics

An interesting observation can be made by looking at the ocean's top predator. Larger oceanic sharks have been moulded by evolution and physics to achieve the perfect hydrodynamic profile. With the bull shark for example, its widest part is found 1/3 of the way down the body, starting from the head. Typically, this width is then 1/5 of the shark's total length.

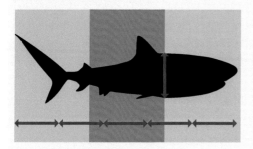

It would be a little on the extreme side to attempt to mould ourselves into shark-like shapes in order to become better freediving photographers. It may affect our social lives too. However, we don't need to rely on nature and evolution to improve our shape, and it is good to have more than one incentive if there's benefit in shedding a few pounds.

Equipment Configuration

Given that we can't all have the perfect body shape, we can take heart in knowing that the real savings to be made in streamlining relate to equipment configuration. Let's start at the top and work downwards.

We know from *Chapter 1: Freediving Equipment for Underwater Photography* that the mask and snorkel induce extra drag, and the snorkel more so.

Assuming you have lead weight around your hips, then this will add some degree of drag. Although not easy to find, some spearfishing and freediving outlets stock smaller flush weights. For someone needing 4 kg of ballast, it is better to wear four 1 kg weights than two 2 kg. This is simply because the heavier weights take up more space and protrude more from the body.

If your weight belt is a Marseillaise type (i.e. long rubber strip), you could be tempted to cut off the excess at the end; after all it would reduce drag. This would compromise safety though, as it makes a quick release more difficult. Better to form a tight loop with the extra and tuck it part way into the band around your middle (as shown in *Chapter 1: Freediving Equipment for Underwater Photography*). Don't forget, we are trying to reduce drag where we can, but it isn't possible to completely eliminate it and, certainly, you must never compromise where your safety is concerned.

You would be forgiven for imagining that fins don't really count, given their constant movement. This is not the case. Imagine a fin travelling through the water of its own accord, foot pocket foremost. As long as the blade is flat, the fin shape isn't going to make a lot of difference as it travels forwards all the while it remains flat within the plane it is travelling. But put a human foot into it and make the foot and leg generate propulsion, then the fin will need to angle up and down with alternate strokes. At brief points during finning, this angle can be nearly perpendicular to the direction of movement and not providing propulsion. It actually provides a counter force, or water brake, albeit for a split second.

A broad blade is going to provide a higher resistance to propulsion ratio than something longer and narrower. When we look at competition freediving fins compared to snorkelling or scuba fins, this is precisely what we find — a long and slightly narrower blade. The fins that are made of carbon fibre rather than thermoplastic polymer are also thinner in substance, reducing drag further.

These days we rarely see top competitive freedivers wearing bifins. The norm is to see athletes using a single-bladed monofin. These are designed to provide maximum thrust. However, in the world of underwater photography, being manoeuvrable is preferable to raw speed. There is further discussion on this topic in *Chapter 6: Finning*.

The Politics of Manoeuvring and Positioning

Now we explore the finning action itself. We have looked at the subject of finning earlier, so while this is a re-iteration it is relative to the subject

The more force that goes into a fin kick, the higher the legs go. The higher the legs go, the higher the drag coefficient. The net result will be higher speed, but this will be at the cost of higher oxygen consumption. Remember the mantra, 'The harder we work, the sooner we need to surface; the sooner we surface, the fewer photographic opportunities we make'.

Conversely we know that too little force, while it will minimise drag, may provide too little propulsion to get to where the action is. So it is a trade-off between generating *momentum* and being *streamlined*. Very often, getting this right is a case of finding what feels about the right amount of momentum and then easing off a little — perhaps about ten percent. We all have a natural desire to want to return to the surface to breathe, and this results in a subconscious tendency to move more quickly than we realise. This is why we need to be a touch slower than the rate that feels correct. It does vary from person to person though.

Arms are without a doubt the biggest challenge with streamlining, especially when you are dangling a camera rig from one or both of them. You need to imagine looking at another freediver finning toward you and where their arms might be, so that the least surface area is visible to your eye. If the approaching freediver was carrying a small form system without strobes, then both arms in a relaxed position, in-line and close to the hips may work. However, this can in some people be destabilising and the cause of hip-rolling, resulting in inefficient finning. For a larger rig that needs to be held with both hands, then arms forward and camera in front of the head and shoulders is the best position. Elbows need to be as straight as possible.

Arms at side

Arms fore

Keep that imaginary approaching freediver in mind and what you should see in front of you is a housed camera with a pair of eyes peering just over the top.

Front view

Technique

If you are finning horizontally, you will of course be looking where you are going. So your neck will be arched back. The neck arching will extend down into the back and that too will arch. Your head will then be prominent above your arched bodyline. So actually, not only does this stress the lower back but it isn't very hydrodynamic at all.

To straighten everything out, the chin set at ninety degrees to the neck is the theoretical solution, although not a practical one. Moving horizontally this would mean looking straight down at the seabed, or into the abyss, rather than ahead. As always there is a compromise. This time it is a combined head and eye tilt. By tilting the head back by about thirty degrees and then rolling your eyes upward, you should then have the forward vision you need without as much drag. Your back will be easier to straighten as well.

Equalising the ears will position the upper arm and elbow into the oncoming flow, and add drag. But it has to be done! You can minimise the duration though, by making descents as vertical as possible. Keeping the elbow tucked in will help too.

Leaving Tension at the Surface

When water meets air surface tension comes into play. Without going into deep physics we can think of this as a skin, and something that needs extra effort to propel through. This will slow down the surface swimmer, and that's before other factors such as waves or surf come into the equation. With all other factors being equal (current, freediver physiology, equipment, etc.), then a freediver underwater is more efficient than one swimming on the surface.

It is not uncommon for freediving photographers to want to find an intersecting point underwater, where a subject such as a turtle or whale shark will pass by. By placing one's self at this junction, a good vantage point can be gained without resorting to chasing the creature. What I tend to notice though is that the photographer will usually put in maximum effort by swimming at the surface, before reaching and then descending to this target point. Very often they are not fast enough, or only have enough breath-hold to last a few seconds.

Instead they could make an immediate descent and then swim to the desired location underwater, minimising effort and maximising efficiency.

One last point I would make on this subject is to be aware that your surface support freediver is unlikely to be able to keep up with your underwater pace.

It is good to keep their positioning in the back of your mind, should their assistance be needed.

Buoyancy Factors

There is a close association between neutral buoyancy and hydrodynamic efficiency. As discussed earlier, the very action of your fin kick induces drag. If your state of buoyancy is anything other than neutral, this will be compounded. A positively buoyant freediver will naturally have their body tilted downward, in an attempt to oppose positive lift. Therefore the view of their oncoming cross-section will be larger, meaning more water resistance. The same is true for the over-weighted freediver, except their tilt or attitude in the water will be head up as they attempt to oppose negative buoyancy. A neutrally buoyant freediver moving horizontally will have the smallest cross-section, and be more hydrodynamic than one that is too light or too heavy.

Under-weighted diver (most typically observed)

Overweighted diver (and safety concern)

Correctly weighted diver (now optimally hydrodynamic)

You may now be able to build a picture of the most efficient route to a particular point underwater. Let's say that point is fifteen metres away and five metres down. Let's also say your neutrally buoyant point is at six metres. The route of maximum efficiency would be a vertical descent to four metres, a horizontal swim to just above your target, and then a final one metre descent. For practical purposes in this example, the horizontal part of the swim could be angled down slightly to make up the final metre. A fully diagonal swim would be an inefficient one, even though in this example it adds up to 15.8 metres, versus twenty metres of square profile distance. Why? Because you would need to equalise for the full 15.8 metres and also that more effort would be spent correcting buoyancy. If you have doubts about this, then it is always something you can try for yourself. Give it a go and experience the difference.

Routing down and across (at a slight downward angle) rather than diagonally will give the freediver a longer stay at the target point.

It is altogether possible that being efficient and making a right angle approach will mean losing sight of a subject, especially if visibility is poor. In these situations be pragmatic and take the direct route!

Practice Makes Perfect

At this point you may be realising that there is a wide gap between what comes naturally to you swimming underwater and what you should be doing to improve efficiency. The other thought you may have, is that you have no idea how your under-water movement looks anyway.

This is where pool training pays off, especially within an established freediving club. You should be able to find someone with whom you can take turns analysing technique. If you have an underwater video (or stills camera with video capability), then ask a volunteer or your buddy to film you.

Saltfree is an outdoor UK freediving club that focuses mainly on depth disci-plines. There are other UK clubs that are run from swimming pools as well.

Most newcomers to freediving have one prominent fault with their style. It may not be the only fault, but will be more obvious than the others — and it could be anything from incorrect head position to hip-rolling, bent knees to arched backs. Whenever I coach someone, I get them to focus on the one dominant fault and spend time correcting it over the course of an hour's session. When we meet again the following week, then that fault should be corrected or will have been improved upon, and we can tackle the next. And so it continues.

Current — May The Force Be With You

Earlier, I briefly mentioned current. This is a subject in its own right, but not one I intend to examine in detail in this chapter. Not because it isn't important, in fact more because it is. The misapprehension of currents and tides is the cause of many maritime incidents.

With respect to hydrodynamics, the effects of current underwater are fairly obvious. Swim headlong into it and you may not travel far or even in the right direction. It is another reason to be as streamlined as possible. There is one technique you may be able to put to good use, should you find yourself pitted against a strong current. If the water you are in is not too deep, then you may find that swimming closer to the bottom makes life a little easier as there will generally be less current there, and the topography can break up the flow.

Equipment Configuration II

Quite clearly your camera equipment will slow you down, and needless to say, a large form system will slow you down more than a small form. Hydrodynamic considerations should be made as part of the criteria for choosing a particular set-up.

Your biggest hydrodynamic enemy is likely to be a strobe, or more specifically, strobes plus their arms. These can turn your underwater imaging equipment into an unwieldy lattice of metal and plastic, providing an extremely efficient water-brake. If strobes are to be used, then those with thinner arms are best.

The strobe arm shown uppermost is the most hydrodynamic © www.marinfoto.no

Trends come and go. Sometimes natural light or strobe-lit photos are more in vogue. Freedivers turned photographers do seem to be reluctant to use strobes. This probably relates to being accustomed to the experience of carrying little or no equipment. There are certain situations, though, where either it is necessary, or is less of an encumbrance. You may be attempting a 'split-level' image of a reef underwater combined with a sunset, for example. This would need strobe light. On the plus side, it would require little or no hydrodynamic movement, so the strobe should be welcome in that situation.

I prefer to go strobe-free whenever I can, which sometimes has the added advantage of being less stressful/threatening for the subject. It is certainly less stressful for me if there is a current to be dealt with!

There are plenty of other photography accessories that will also cause delay to your underwater movement: focusing torches, auxiliary lenses and their respective lens carriers, lanyards and so on. My approach to the problem is to start with the bare minimum, i.e. camera in housing, and then consider piece by piece what I really need to add to that for the dive. So I would use a lanyard in deep water, but possibly not in an environment where the camera can be easily retrieved if dropped. These situations should be evaluated in their entirety and the best combination chosen accordingly.

It makes sense to take stock and consider if you do actually need to be hydrodynamic on the dive you are undertaking. Some dives can be fairly static with little or no need to venture much below the surface, for example photographing animals such as manatees. On the other hand, even if you are only capturing images at surface level, you may find that travelling from point A to point B is achieved more effectively underwater, and hydrodynamics are therefore still relevant.

Summary

- Consider choice of wetsuit, fins, mask and weights.
- Is a trip to the gym overdue?
- Leave your snorkel at the surface.
- Fin with synchronism and conservatism.
- Arms straight and either by your side or holding your camera rig at head level.
- Keep head and neck in-line with body as much as possible, and tilt eyes upward.
- Straight-down descents rather than on diagonals.
- Find near-neutral buoyancy for horizontal swims.
- Surface swims use more energy than when swimming submerged.
- Train/be filmed at a freediving pool session.
- Correct faults in style one at a time.
- Consider hydrodynamics when choosing/configuring camera equipment.
- If you don't *need* to move you don't *need* to be hydrodynamic!

Technique

Is this freediver in trouble, or just exhaling for comfort?:
a decision for their partner to make © Laura Storm/Planet Plankton
[Canon EOS 550D with Sigma 10–20mm lens, SEA&SEA housing, f6.3 at 1/160s, ISO 400]

Safety

'I cannot conceive of any vital disaster happening to this vessel.
Modern shipbuilding has gone beyond that'

Captain E J Smith (Captain of the Titanic) [1]

Freediving courses and manuals take the competitive line, where they expect freedivers to push limits, and therefore blackouts are inevitable — rescues will be needed. In this book advice has been provided to extend underwater time by cumulative improvement techniques, but safety has been taken into account at every step — there is deliberately no suggestion to push limits. However, the concentration that goes into photography could distract a freediver from self-monitoring, so we need to establish guidelines that can be used to counteract this.

Being in the water carries increased risk. It is why we have lifeguards at public swimming pools but not so in parks or playgrounds, for example. If we see someone in trouble at a swimming pool, we can elect to call the lifeguards and leave rescuing to those trained to carry it out. In open water not only do the risks increase (exposure, current, depth, marine life, etc.), but there may not be a nominee whose job and responsibility is the rescue of others.

At this point then, you may be considering either your own safety, that of those around you, or hopefully both. We will look at some of the risks to ourselves and others, and what we can do to mitigate these. Rescue techniques are not appropriate for inclusion — **the only acceptable way to learn how to perform in-water rescue is on an approved training course**, where it can be properly demonstrated, practiced, and tested.

---

1   Of course, this quote wasn't actually about the *Titanic*, but some years previous, perhaps making it even more relevant — do not be complacent!

Technique

You will find the following messages repeated throughout this book:

· Never venture offshore on your own.

· In no circumstances freedive without someone alongside you.

· Freediving techniques should be learned on an approved training course.

These principles are fundamental to mitigation of many (though not all) of the risks that can be faced.

Hypoxia

Low levels of oxygen in the bloodstream, with blue tinged de-oxygenated blood causing colour changes visible in the lips, nail beds and head area (cyanosis). *There may be no symptoms experienced by the person concerned, so a diver showing these signs should always be informed.*

Freediver showing signs of cyanosis

Technique

Loss of Motor Control (LMC)

A semi-conscious state where the individual has uncontrollable tremors, shaking and/ or twitching. Typically observed in the arms, legs and shoulders. This is sometimes referred to as 'samba'. It is a manifestation of advanced hypoxia and frequently progresses to a blackout.

Blackout

Full loss of consciousness. Can be preceded or accompanied by LMC. The head may arch back and muscles become rigid. Eyes may be open, and the sufferer may make vocal noises. After returning to consciousness, the victim frequently has no memorable experience of the event, or of a short time beforehand. Because of this, often there is a denial that anything abnormal has actually taken place.

Hypoxia and Blackout

Let's look firstly at some of the more serious risks in open water. This is particularly relevant to the underwater photographer, who may be paying more attention to photography than his or her physiology. For the freediver, first and foremost lies the risk of hypoxia leading to loss of motor control and blackout. An unrescued blackout victim in the water usually drowns. Freedivers I have known who have drowned died due to not being rescued from blackout. In freediving competitions, any athlete who experiences blackout normally makes a full recovery, due to the fact that teams of safety divers are on standby to initiate a rescue.

There are a number of significant influences leading to hypoxia, and the top three are:

1.   Hyperventilation.
2.   Diving too deeply (i.e. beyond the diver's experience).
3.   Dive duration too long (also beyond the diver's experience).

Hyperventilation is covered in more detail in *Chapter 5: Lungcraft*. If we assume that we are sensible enough to avoid doing this altogether, then how do we gauge the other two? In my experience, I would be surprised to see an established freediver perform a five metre dive for thirty seconds and subsequently suffer an hypoxic event. I would likewise be surprised to see an inexperienced freediver perform a thirty metre dive for two minutes, and *not* suffer an hypoxic event. Unfortunately there is a lot of latitude between these two extremes.

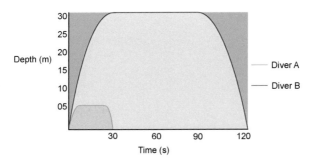

Diver A is trained and experienced. Diver B is inexperienced. With diver A, hypoxic issues are unlikely; with diver B, issues are probable. The grey area between the two extremes is significant: either situation could occur in this zone.

Glass and Water

With a dive duration that is too long, there is some avoidance potential. If you are not exceptionally deep (i.e. less than ten metres), and the urge to breathe becomes noticeable, then surfacing at this point will reduce the risk.

With diving too deeply, increasing depth causes increasing partial pressures of all component gases, and our warning mechanisms cope less well with this. In other words, you can do a deep dive and feel little urge to breathe, yet metabolise a significant quantity of oxygen.

When ascending, lung volume will increase and gas partial pressures decrease. If oxygen partial pressures are too low (due to metabolic usage), then oxygen bonding to haemoglobin in the bloodstream is weakened and this becomes another contributing factor to blackout. When blackout occurs on the ascent as described here, it is referred to as *shallow water blackout*.

So far this paints a confusing picture of how to determine potential blackouts and, unfortunately, that's pretty much the point.

A trained, experienced freediver will have practiced enough to know their own physiological profile, and how deep they can go for how long. This can also be counter-effective, as a false reliance can be made on these values, so that safety principles are then disregarded.

I believe that mitigation should consist of the following four-step plan:

1. Adhere to the 'Fundamental Freediving Safety Principles' outlined earlier in this chapter.
2. Take into account the three previously listed primary hypoxia influences.
3. Through further training and practice, build your own depth/time profile and keep well within its limits.
4. Understand the signs and symptoms of hypoxia.

Signs of hypoxia in others may consist of bluish lips, fingernails, scalp and neck … if you are able to see these. Staring eyes, uncontrollable twitching, jerky movements and unexplained strange behaviour all mean the onset of loss of motor control. During a dive, you could see your partner become limp, or uncoordinated and spinning around the guide line. There may be a sudden exhalation of air, and/or the head jerking to one side. A general lack of direction, arms splaying out, or failure to return pre-arranged signals are also indicators.

Freediver showing signs of shallow water blackout

In yourself the symptoms can range from ringing in the ears, visual disturbance, tunnel vision, changes to perception of time, or some other unusual sensory experience (perhaps feeling warmer than usual). These symptoms can be very subtle though or absent altogether. If in doubt, then surface immediately.

When your partner dives you should remain on the surface at all times, unless they are performing a longer or deeper dive. In this case you should dive down and meet them for the last five to ten metres of their ascent. During this period and just after surfacing, monitor their condition carefully. The majority of blackouts occur on surfacing, or just before. If accompanying your partner for the latter stages of their dive, then have your camera equipment secured elsewhere. Either that, or don't be precious about letting go of it if you are involved in a rescue.

Following a successful rescue, if the recovery from blackout has been swift, then diving for both partners should cease for the day. Some time spent analysing the cause is time well spent, as it may be something that can be prevented in future. If the blackout lasts more than thirty seconds or there are other medical issues, then seek out a physician when you return to shore (if you are in any doubt, then do this anyway).

The bottom line with hypoxia and blackouts is that they can still occur despite the four-step prevention plan. But the first step will mean that either you or your partner are trained and ready to activate a rescue.

Barotrauma

Barotrauma is physical damage to body tissues caused by a difference in pressure between a gas space inside or in contact with the body, and the surrounding fluid. This is another risk to the freediver rather than a surface snorkeller, but more manageable than hypoxic blackout.

It can manifest anywhere that air exists next to or within the body.

The most serious aspect to consider is 'lung squeeze'. This can happen on dives where the space in the lungs reduces so much that a vacuum effect ensues, and blood capillaries rupture. Reduced air volume in the throat can have a similar effect, and can be exacerbated by the diver flexing the neck by looking downwards. The result of either of these conditions is blood pooling in the lungs. It is also likely to bring forward the likelihood of hypoxia as an unwelcome side-effect. In very rare cases it can be fatal.

I have never observed lung squeeze in freedivers staying above ten metres, provided they have taken a full breath of air before the dive. In one case I have seen someone suffer from this at about fifteen metres, but I believe there may have been an underlying throat condition that contributed in that instance. In most other cases, it generally tends to appear past a depth of twenty-five metres.

The symptoms are an urge to cough anytime during the ascent onward, and at the surface for the coughing to produce blood. Diving should cease until the diver has been tended to by a physician. If there is difficulty in breathing or loss of consciousness, then this becomes an emergency situation and immediate medical attention should be summoned.

It is fair to say that lung squeeze is more common in competitive freediving than in recreational freediving. To reduce the risk, avoid excessively deep dives.

Much further down the severity scale but far more common, is ear squeeze. This is caused by poor or late equalisation, and/or a tight hood sealing against the ear. A build-up of external pressure flexes the eardrum inward unless an equal air pressure from the Eustachian tube counteracts this. Pain is usually felt (though not always), and if not corrected the pressure will eventually rupture the eardrum.

Technique

If a hood is too tight and seals against the ear, then equalisation becomes a complex issue. An easy solution is to carefully punch a small hole in the hood where the ear canal exits.

Improving ear equalisation is covered in *Chapter 7: Descents and Ascents*, but even good technique can occasionally be insufficient. Congestion may prevent the flow of air through to the middle ear. Also, repeated diving can irritate and inflame our tubes to the same effect. Clearly, if we dive with 'sticky tubes' then we risk eardrum rupture. There are avoidance tips in *Chapter 7*.

Sinus squeeze consists of a painful pressure build-up in the sinuses, which may be followed by a bloody discharge. Sometimes the discharge clears the condition and further diving is possible, sometimes not. Congestion from colds and flu are a common cause here. Allergies and hay fever can also contribute to this condition.

Tooth squeeze is where a small crack in a tooth allows air pressure to irritate an exposed nerve. If there is an underlying cavity, this can have unfortunate consequences. The tooth can either implode or explode, depending on the pressure direction, although this is not a common occurrence. Sometimes a minor sinus squeeze can give almost identical symptoms to an upper tooth squeeze.

Mask squeeze is more common with inexperienced divers, who simply forget to exhale a little air into the mask space while descending. The suction can rupture small capillaries in the eyes, making them bloodshot.

Compressed gas

Very often freedivers and scuba divers will be on the same dive site at the same time. Some freedivers like to impress scuba divers with their breath-hold abilities, and this can lead to avoidable incidents. More significantly though, sometimes scuba divers offer freedivers air from their tanks. **This is definitely to be avoided**. It carries the real risk of pulmonary embolism. If a freediver were to be unable to ascend for some reason, and absolutely *had* to breathe compressed air underwater, then they should continue to share the air source throughout the scuba diver's controlled ascent, along with any requisite safety stop(s). Not doing so would risk injury caused by a rate of ascent (and expanding gas) likely to be far greater than that which is safe following breathing of compressed gas underwater.

With all barotrauma incidents, avoidance is straightforward; avoid descending until the issue is resolved. Depth increases pressure and increased pressure is the cause of barotrauma.

Marine Traffic

Boat traffic is a significant threat, whether freediving or snorkelling. For the freediver certainly this is higher risk, as we are usually invisible to marine traffic while submerged. If a boat engine increases in volume during a dive, it is almost impossible to tell where it is coming from or where it is headed. Being partnered reduces the risk (as long as you are not simultaneously submerged), as does a diver's flag attached to a float. In any case, it pays to be vigilant as even the display of a diver's flag is no guarantee. Before setting out to sea, be aware of shipping lines, sailing routes and other established areas of boat traffic. All should be avoided if possible. If there's one form of marine traffic I try to steer clear of more than any other, it is the jet ski. These can be operated by those with little experience, and usually travel at high speed.

The North American 'diver down' flag is shown left, and the international equivalent on the right is the alpha flag. The American red and white version is more visible from a distance.

Temperature

Wearing a wetsuit that is too thin, or being in the water too long will increase the risk of hypothermia. Eating too little too long before a dive also decreases your tolerance to low temperature. Remember that water is a very efficient conductor of heat away from the body — some twenty times faster than air. Once the shiver reflex sets in, then the ability to breath-hold is severely diminished. Get to know your wetsuit's thermal abilities, and the temperature of the water in which you dive. Tailor-made two-piece open-cell freediving suits, offer better thermal insulation than off-the-peg scuba suits of the same thickness. Also consider what sort of photographic activity you will be involved in. If there is lots of swimming involved, then your metabolism will increase body temperature. If you are fairly static, though, then you will be more vulnerable to low temperature.

Muscular Issues

Muscle fatigue, cramp and/or injury are all interlinked, as they will typically relate to the muscles in your legs. The neck and shoulders can be vulnerable in some people, when travelling in high speed inflatables over choppy seas. With leg muscles there are a number of contributing factors. Highest on the list is insufficient stretching. Swimming at full burst with a camera is an athletic activity, so take athletic precautions! A fin blade that is too stiff is a common cause of cramp, and you may therefore need a softer blade. Many freediving fins have blades and foot pockets that separate, so you may not have to sacrifice your comfortable foot pockets. Cold water will also cause muscles to tense, so warming them with a good pre-dive stretch routine will counteract this. Relieving muscular cramps in the leg is covered in *Chapter 6: Finning*.

Devising a comprehensive stretch routine could
prevent weeks of remedial physiotherapy

Decompression Sickness

Unfortunately there is no such thing as a freediving decompression table, nor a freediving computer that can display recommended safe diving intervals. If you freedive deeply enough and frequently enough, then DCS (the 'bends') can occur. It isn't a common event, and typically would only affect someone performing frequent dives below ten metres over a couple of hours. So although I wouldn't expect this from most freediving photographers, of course, it can't be ruled out. Your photography session may be in just these conditions.

One definite exclusion is mixing scuba and freediving on the same trip. A scuba dive will leave nitrogen dissolved in the body blood and tissue compartments for several hours after surfacing. A rapid descent and ascent, as is typical on a freedive, can easily cause this dissolved nitrogen to emerge from solution in the form of bubbles. The safest rule you can follow here is via your dive computer (see *Chapter 1: Freediving Equipment for Underwater Photography*) — if the no-fly icon is still present on the computer display after your scuba diving, then avoid freediving.

After scuba diving, better not to freedive until the no-fly warning has cleared.

Overhead Environments

Entering a shipwreck or cave, where it is no longer possible to make a vertical ascent, is defined as an overhead environment. The same is true for freediving beneath ice. This poses more risk for a number of reasons:

1. The route to the surface may be ambiguous or not obvious.
2. There is likely to be much less ambient light.
3. There is the potential for silt to obscure the way out.
4. Physical entrapment can happen in a confined area.

Scuba diving in overhead environments can be hazardous, and those that undertake it do so with the appropriate equipment and specialist training (or at least should do). Reels, torches, staging cylinders and protective equipment are fairly standard, and multiple items are carried for redundancy. It doesn't seem a sensible option for the freediver to enter overhead environments, but I am aware that it is becoming more popular, especially with respect to cavern freediving.

Glass and Water

Looking at overhead environment freediving in the context of underwater photography, I can only put forward the opinion that **I don't believe it to be a sensible mixture**. In addition to the risks just mentioned, you then have to add in the complexity and distraction of handling camera equipment, not to mention the challenges of trying to capture images or video footage in low light conditions.

This sort of freediving requires specialist training over and above a basic course. If you are resolute in combining photography while freediving in an overhead environment, then at least gain some (partnered) experience in doing so without your camera.

Other Considerations

There are some risks that aren't worth mentioning due to their improbability, and some that should have obvious ways to reduce them. With the latter, worth mentioning are: tides and current, dehydration, sun exposure, entrance/exit hazards, panic attack, fatigue, hitting a hard object while ascending or descending, freediving at night, aggressive marine life, loss or damage to equipment, trespassing on private property, and flooding the bag that contains the electronic key fob for your car! With a little prior thought, planning and/or care these are all avoidable.

Self Rescue

Consider for a moment a scenario where you have dived down to photograph a moving subject. Your partner monitors you closely from the surface. You are concentrating on getting the right image, but all the while the subject draws you deeper, and you lose perception of the passing time. Your partner looks back to check where your boat is, but when he puts his face back in the water he can no longer see you. Suddenly you realise you are negatively buoyant, and starting to sink, and now you are starting to experience tunnel vision. No need to continue further; you get the picture. When the mistakes of two humans intersect, the outcome can be catastrophic.

The Freedivers Recovery Vest (FRV) is an inflatable jacket with small compressed gas cartridges and an electronics unit incorporated. The wearer programmes a target depth and time into the electronics interface. If either of these are exceeded during the dive, unless manually overridden the jacket will self-inflate and lift the diver to the surface. Gas bladders are positioned such that the diver floats face-up, ready for surface rescue. This is a very simple explanation; there are other additional safety features included.

Inevitably, wearing an FRV will mean extra drag to some degree, however the device is low-profile and snug fitting. If you have streamlined yourself by using the techniques and equipment described elsewhere in this book, then you won't particularly undo the improvements there. As with carrying your camera rig, it will just be an offsetting factor.

Introducing a second backup mechanism is more than just a prudent measure. Sky divers have reserve parachutes. Freedivers who compete have a double backup system, and those that set sled depth records have at least three.[2] To make a point, how many copies of your images do you make?

FRV in normal use (uninflated) © Terry Maas, Oceanic Safety Systems LLC

---

2   Otherwise known as 'No Limits' the use of a weighted sled enables competitors to descend as deep as possible and then use a small gas cylinder to inflate a balloon and return to the surface.

Glass and Water

Summary

Taking a camera underwater can be a distraction to the hazards around us. So we should be mindful of those hazards beforehand, and give thought to how best to deal with them. Even more importantly we should consider how to prevent them in the fist instance. Key points here:

- Always be partnered, and learn how to rescue others.
- Hyperventilation, diving too deeply and staying under too long increase the risk of blacking out.
- Know the signs and symptoms of hypoxia.
- Avoid depths where barotraumas become an issue.
- A diver flag highlights your presence to boat traffic.
- Shivering vastly reduces breath-hold ability.
- A good stretch routine will reduce the potential for cramp.
- Overhead environments require specialist training.
- To avoid DCS, do not mix scuba and freediving on dive trips.
- To avoid serious lung injury, do not breathe air from scuba equipment while freediving.
- The Freedivers Recovery Vest provides an additional safety net, but doesn't replace a rescue-trained partner.

Technique

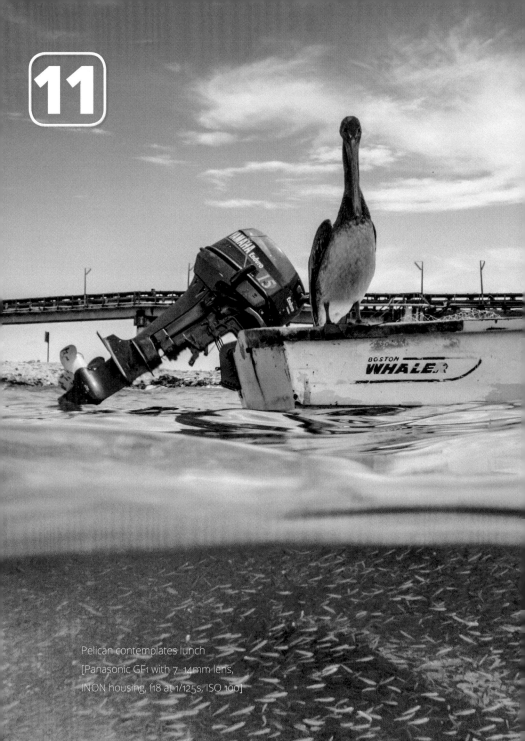

Pelican contemplates lunch
[Panasonic GF1 with 7-14mm lens,
INON housing, f18 at 1/125s, ISO 100]

Creature By Creature

> 'An understanding of the natural world and what's in it is a
> source of not only a great curiosity but great fulfillment'
>
> *Sir David Attenborough*

When we photograph wildlife underwater, in many cases we are not simply casual observers. Whether we intend to or not, we often initiate interaction with the creatures we seek out. On land this doesn't always happen, as many wildlife photographers want to capture natural behaviour and so use 'hides', vehicles and long lenses to create a barrier.

For the underwater photographer it is a bit trickier attempting to look like a lump of coral in order to blend in with the surroundings. The further we are from the subject the more water we end up having to photograph through, and as covered in *Chapter 3: Underwater Photography Basics* that creates its own problems. So, we accept that we will be seen and hopefully tolerated. How we behave and interact often dictates how the subject will react, and what type of image we end up capturing. This chapter is about these behaviours and interactions.

The primary consideration above all else should be the health and well-being of the animals on both sides of the lens. An animal being stressed or harassed is not worth the (generally inferior) image that will be produced. If it puts you at risk as well, then that is equally questionable. I am sure we have all seen video footage where 'dangerous' animals are being provoked until or near the point where they defend themselves. I certainly don't see it as a natural encounter. The other end of the spectrum would be an animal left alone in its environment, away from any human presence. So when we enter the water and make an approach to an animal, we position ourselves somewhere between these two extremes. This is something that should be reviewed and considered at all times.

I try to adopt the principle of the three R's — Research, Regulations and Respect. There's little excuse for not finding out about the animal you are studying or filming, and I believe (or hope) that most of us do at least some research beforehand. Sometimes there are legal regulations and recommendations and these should be observed too: they are there for good reason. Beyond these two principles is the straightforward respect and commonsense we should apply. Laws and species knowledge are not always sufficient protection; sometimes additional thought and care for good measure is in order.

The 'leave only bubbles' philosophy is a righteous one, and worth subscribing to. Unfortunately our mere presence in the water prevents it from being absolute. Perhaps if we think more of ourselves as visitors to someone else's home, and remember to 'take our shoes off before treading on the carpet' then that would help.

For many scuba divers these considerations are often left for the resident dive guide to deliver as part of the dive brief (although these can vary in quality and detail). As a freediver it is more common (by comparison) for you to be in an environment without a guide. So the research and consideration may become your responsibility.

Different marine creatures require varying approaches if we want to win their confidence and not scare or provoke them. Here are a few tips that other contributors and I can share our experience of.

West Indian Manatee

A marine mammal that rarely shows signs of aggression is the West Indian manatee. This has been to its detriment, and mankind has pushed this species to the edge of extinction. Today it is still under threat from toxic red tides, thermal shock and collision with pleasure boats. West Indian manatees live around the coastal regions of Florida and The Bahamas, and in the winter months seek warmer waters in waterways and inlets fed by thermal springs. This brings them into conflict with boat traffic. Many manatees show wounds inflicted from boat propellers, and not all survive. We have a duty to look after these gentle creatures, and that includes how we interact with them.

It is becoming more common (and profitable) for boat operators to dump boatfuls of snorkellers into the manatees' frequented waterways. They then become habituated to human contact and their feeding and sleeping patterns are disturbed. The Florida Fish and Wildlife Conservation Commission has tight regulations about manatee interaction, and they are carefully monitored in certain areas … but not all.

Glass and Water

Manatees should never be approached — let them decide if they want to take that initiative. Sometimes they will not only approach, but may actually nuzzle up to you. Although there is the ensuing temptation to hug them or scratch their tummies, this is discouraged. There is no need to push them away, but don't encourage an ongoing relationship! From a photographic point of view, close interactions won't help you obtain good images as you really will be too near.

If they are resting or feeding they should not be disturbed at all (which includes swimming over the top of a resting manatee). There are also ring-fenced sanctuary areas for them in the more populated areas, and these must not be entered into.

Other restrictions include: not diving underneath them; not separating a mother from its calf; times of day when interaction is allowed; and when you are allowed to use strobes (check with the local authorities on this as it may vary). For my own part, my preference is to take the challenge of using natural light and avoiding use of a strobe feels less intrusive too. They are found in shallow water anyway. If you are using strobes, then don't use them repeatedly, and avoid repositioning them (this is because manatees are sensitive to high-pitched noise, and moving strobe arm joints can cause them to squeal).

Be aware that water temperatures in Florida waterways can be quite chilly during the winter months. So can air temperatures, and on rare occasions there can be frosts. So combined with a possible early start, and being in an environment where you are less likely to be moving around, your thermal protection can be compromised. I have used a two-piece 3mm wetsuit before, and found it to provide insufficient warmth.

Manatees are often static or slow moving, although not always. So combined with good light and clear water, they make for great photographic subjects.

Sea Lions

Imagine the zaniest, crazy animated cartoon you can, and then translate this into a marine environment that you are part of. This is what it is like trying to photograph sealions underwater. One predictable aspect of photographing sealions is this: they are unpredictable! They have a habit of ignoring the rules of conduct we expect from them.

Although they will throw away your rule book, the one sensible guideline you should observe is to steer well clear of the alpha male. He is bigger than you are, he knows it, and he likes to remind you and his female entourage that he's in charge. He is easy to spot — larger than the others, with a prominent forehead, and by barking and blowing bubbles will generally make his presence felt. He has an uncompromising view of his territory, so **keep your distance**.

The other reason that it is difficult to apply guidelines when swimming with sea lions is that (in my experience) each colony has its own set of behavioural patterns. Some are shy, some not, and others generally uninterested in human presence. Human habituation and breeding / feeding cycles play a part in this, but you can certainly observe differences between one colony and another on a given day.

With the less interactive groups you will have random opportunities to capture images. If they are in a playful mood, but only with each other, then the behaviour you capture will be more natural. You will find that they will happily make toys out of sticks, starfish, and other loose objects (living or not!). They will toss these around to each other, bring them to the surface in order to let them sink … and then repeat the whole sequence again.

My experience of sea lions that choose to interact with humans is more akin to the cartoon scenario described earlier. The interaction is most definitely on their terms and can comprise 'fly pasts'… with rapid twists and turns, somersaults, and pirouettes. Anything to make your movements look clumsy and ineffective.

As high a shutter speed as possible is best in order to get those 'peak-of-action' shots. Don't be surprised to find a snout pressed up against your dome port! Be prepared to capture images at different depths, not just at the surface, although bear in mind the best natural light will be in the shallows. Strobes may help with creative shots if you have an appetite for freezing motion blur with a 'rear-curtain sync' flash setting. Rear-curtain sync is where the camera fires

Glass and Water

the flash burst just before the shutter closes (rather than just after it opens, which makes the motion blur appear in the wrong direction, i.e. ahead of the subject).

Sometimes sea lions can get a little over-boisterous. They don't generally bite maliciously, but I have seen playful nips draw blood. So do exercise some caution, and as always don't initiate any physical contact yourself.

Seals

In many respects interactions with seals are similar to those with sea lions. Certainly, those colonies that are more

Freediver and Californian sea lion

exposed to human contact (for example scuba divers) tend to have individuals that approach more closely or interact more freely. For them to take an interest in you, it seems to work better if you don't take an interest in them. Also, they like to have space in which they can manoeuvre away from you. An ideal position is to find a clump of kelp a few metres down and hang alongside this, nearby to the seal(s).

It has been suggested but I don't think there is any firm evidence to prove it that freedivers have more or better interactions with seals and sea lions over and above those using scuba. However, we know that being near the surface means that natural light is more in abundance, and photographic variables become more flexible in this zone. My perception of my own images captured using both methods, is that photographing while freediving has produced much more dynamic shots. Being faster and more manoeuvrable also helps with the business of placing a fast-moving animal in the frame.

Dolphins

My in-water experience with dolphins relates predominantly to bottlenose and Atlantic spotted dolphin. Both species are well-known for their gregarious nature. The bottlenose sometimes produces individuals who leave their family groups and become lone wanderers, and there have been cases where some of these go on to seek human contact. Very rarely, this can be of benefit to both the dolphin and the individual or human community they become part of. That is a highly idealistic view and in most cases the reverse happens. It is more common for the dolphin interaction to be monetised, the dolphin becomes exploited and ends up being injured or driven away.

We need to think about the dolphins' priorities when we enter the water with them. They need to eat, breathe, sleep and breed. If they don't need to play

then certainly they like to, but that's lower down the list of these priorities. So don't assume that your presence will instantly divert them from whatever they were doing to taking an interest in you. They can quite happily perform their daily activities with complete disregard for humans with cameras bobbing around on the surface. By far the majority of encounters I have experienced have consisted of a fleeting glimpse of a pod travelling from one location to another. In those circumstances, the only acknowledgement I have received has been the odd wink or flick of the tail. The Douglas Adams phrase of 'so long and thanks for all the fish' strikes a chord.

On the occasions where interaction has taken place, I have found it to be a

Atlantic spotted dolphin

Glass and Water

rewarding experience. If they are in a playful mood then they will play ball with you … if you play ball with them.

The more you can emulate dolphin behaviour by twisting and turning underwater and generally finning alongside the pod, then the more interest the dolphins seem to take. They are curious, intelligent animals that respond well to being entertained, but equally seem to lose interest if something more appealing catches their eye.

If you are in the water as a spectator, remaining still at the surface peering through your viewfinder, then the dolphins are less likely to interact and will probably move on. I think that keeping detached is a safer and less intrusive option, and also aligned to comments I have made earlier. Additionally there is no doubt that your photography will suffer if you decide to interact. It is just that if there is nothing to amuse a group of dolphins, then generally speaking they have better things to go and do. If you can find a willing 'dolphin wrangler', then he or she can provide the needed entertainment and act as a model too.

Do not reach out to touch or hug a dolphin and **never put your hands near their blow holes**. Don't forget as well, these are large powerful animals with sharp teeth. Despite their smiling rostrums, this doesn't mean you aren't face-to-face with an angry or disturbed individual. Or a male that wants to mate and isn't being too selective about gender or species. Bottlenose dolphins can sometimes be downright bullies.

Personally, I'd only go out with the intention of photographing dolphins when there is boat cover present. You may need to make a swift exit to avoid personal injury and/or psychological scars. Being bullied or harassed by dolphins isn't common behaviour, but it is possible.

As with photographing sea lions, a high shutter speed will improve sharpness (unless you want to show motion blur). If you are performing the dual role of entertainer and photographer, be mindful of your own changes in depth and position, and how this affects light coming into the camera. You could otherwise end up with incorrect exposures. Also, do apply some thought to exertion and its impact on your breath-hold. Tempting as it will be to try and keep up with a playful pod, overdoing things will shorten successive dives. Replace enthusiasm with grace and style! Where water is shallow (i.e. five to ten metres) and the bottom sandy, then be aware that bright sunlight will bounce upward from this and have a significant bearing on exposure. Bright sunshine and a sandy bottom will mean that you are well placed to increase shutter speed without having to increase ISO, so look on this as a benefit.

Long-finned Pilot Whale
by Andrew Sutton

Long-finned pilot whale pod © Andrew Sutton

As with any assignment, research your subject and get to know behaviour patterns of the whales. If you are planning to photograph pilot whales, you are hopefully an accomplished freediver and photographer; this is emphatically not an environment for beginners: these are large, agile, highly intelligent hunters.

Pilot whales are large, oceanic dolphins (like orca or killer whales), and can be found around the central warmer waters of the globe. They are toothed whales with a bulbous head and are predominantly black with white belly markings. They live in social groups and the young are often nurse-maided by older females. Pilot whales, like orca, hunt in packs and have been called the 'cheetah of the sea' due to the speed at which they can dive and stalk prey (typically squid). They are extremely vocal and communicate with complex clicks and whistles.

On several occasions, I've witnessed some heart-stopping warning signs, whereby an individual or small group of 'outriders' will emerge from the main group to sound you out and issue a warning if they feel threatened in any way. This is usually a single pilot approaching, standing vertically and gyrating. If close, they will often tail slap and 'snap' at you before they speed off, making way for two or three other pod members to appear behind or underneath you. This explicitly displays command of their domain. What should you do? I retreated, tried to make myself small, and got back aboard the boat pretty swiftly!

Chances are you'll be using either a GoPro or DSLR (stills/video), but knowing where the sun is and understanding the light is *the* golden rule. I do not use strobes in this environment as they can cause stress in the animal.

GoPro: Needs no introduction — just mount them securely!

DSLRs: Light, water colour, time of day, planning, luck…! I will usually start my shoot manually with mid-to-high ISO (400–1500), shutter 500 (ish), f4–2. It usually gets good pleasing images. There should be no need to exceed ten metres unless you want descending fluke shots.

- Make sure your vessel is handled responsibly at all times and fully complies with relevant local or national regulations or guidelines governing whale watching or close approach to whales and dolphins.
- Enter the water gently and approach the whale calmly.
- Maintain a safe distance and constant depth.
- Never attempt to touch a whale, for your safety and welfare as well as the whale's (whales have delicate skin which is easily damaged and there is also a small possibility of disease transmission).
- Look out for aggressive or distressed behaviour and remain calm.
- Be aware of young whales being protected by the pod — do not approach them and take special care around mothers with young calves, giving them plenty of space.
- Be aware of the whales' direction of travel. Never chase the animals in a boat or while in the water. Allow them to approach you.
- Try to keep the encounter short and move away after a few minutes. If you're lucky to encounter a heat run, you'll get multiple opportunities to move carefully ahead of the main pod and, again, always be aware that you are a guest in their domain.

I apply these rules to all my work with blue whales, sperm whales and any cetacean I am lucky enough to photograph.

Andrew Sutton is a photojournalist and ambassador for WDC, Whale and Dolphin Conservation. As a photojournalist his work takes him across the globe, and he also runs photo studios in London and Madrid. His published work includes: *The Guardian*, WildlifeExtra.com, BBC (*Ocean Giants*), Philip Hoare (author) and many others. More information at www.whales.org

Sharks

There are many different species of shark in our oceans and many different behavioural patterns. Whale and basking sharks I will deal with separately further on, as the differences here are more specific.

'Man eating shark' may bring to mind a ferocious oceanic predator. Another view of this phrase, is that of humans consuming sharks. This we do at an unsustainable rate. Millions are slaughtered every year to satisfy a demand for one small portion of their anatomy — the fins. Unless this appetite is curbed, we will drive them to extinction and have no opportunity to see sharks in their natural environment.

Freediving with the intention of photographing sharks is questionable if the option to do the same on scuba is present. One of the first principles of any form of shark diving is to be constantly observant. Sharks have a much higher tendency to make an approach if eye contact has not been made. Freedivers have to spend significant periods at the surface, and therefore have two separate mediums to pay attention to. In other words, a freediver may not even see a nearby shark, let alone make eye contact with it. In addition, some species can **confuse a human at the surface with some other form of prey** — a seal for example. These factors therefore place freedivers at some degree of higher risk to shark attack than scuba divers.

With some species I would exercise more caution than others. The great white shark is an obvious contender, but tiger, bull, oceanic white tip and great hammerhead are all examples of sharks that are considered to be more dangerous, by comparison to the remainder.

Tiger shark

So far I have painted a cautionary picture and perhaps one of insecurity around getting in the water with sharks. I should balance this out, as I know there are experienced freedivers who regularly interact with all of the higher risk shark species, including the great white. The people who do this though, usually have an acute awareness of the danger signs to watch out for, and even they take the risk of misinterpretation.

Are there any obvious danger signs? If a shark has arched its back and exaggerates fin flicking, this can be territorial behaviour that may lead to confrontation. Similarly, if a shark is continually circling and/or bumping you then clearly it has developed a level of curiosity that might lead to something more invasive.

I for one, would be more comfortable diving into a school of hammerhead sharks than a school of nesting triggerfish (the latter can have aggressive tendencies when nesting). As always I would avoid making physical contact. Obviously, diving in shark territories that have low visibility or are part of an active feeding ground will increase your risk of an incident.

Your own body language and positioning will have a bearing on how you are perceived. If you were to wildly thrash your hands and arms around, this could attract unwanted attention. Hands should ideally be gloved and tucked in, so that they are not mistaken for food. Eye contact and standing your ground also sends out a message, that you are aware of the shark's presence and may pose a risk to it should it consider an aggressive move.

Regarding the business of how you could photograph sharks, upward angles work well. The larger individuals (or, if you are lucky, schools) can make good silhouettes. A single shark at depth on a sandy bottom can also be a strong image.

One last word of caution — if a shark is getting close to you and you have an acrylic dome port, then try and angle it away. Their skin has abrasive denticles, and they can leave deep scratches!

Whale Sharks/Basking Sharks

These two species of shark are the largest, and in both cases their diet consists mainly of plankton. So, however intimidating their size, they are not known to attack humans.

Basking sharks are found in temperate zones, whereas whale sharks are generally tropical. Because of their diet, the waters in which they feed will often not have good visibility. So this is the first challenge for the photographer.

The next challenge is their speed of travel — it is deceptively fast. The large mass of these creatures can give the impression that they lumber past quite sedately. If they are on the move (rather than feeding), then they will be moving a lot faster than you can. If you do find yourself in a position where you are trying to fin alongside a basking or whale shark, then as covered in *Chapter 9: Hydrodynamics* you will propel yourself faster underwater rather than on the surface.

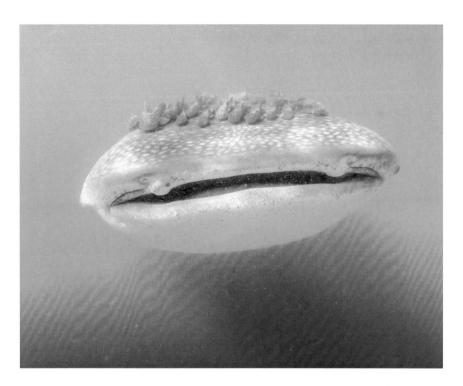

Whale shark hosting a multitude of remora

The classic shot of these imposing fish is coming toward you at a slight angle, mouth agape. Obtaining this will not happen by accident — you need to be correctly positioned beforehand. An experienced boat skipper can track the direction of travel and then manoeuvre ahead to drop you in the path of trajectory. This drop-off point is not the time or place to be playing with camera settings! You may only get the chance of a single shot, and the whale shark will be upon you sooner than you think. So have the camera on with settings pre-programmed (a good example of these can be found in the camera checklist in *Chapter 7: Descents and Ascents*).

Another shot that can work quite nicely is a full silhouette, taken from below — just be sure to block out the sun with the fish. Both basking and whale sharks will frequently be present at the surface (which is helpful), but also be prepared for them to dive. For whale sharks, once I am awaiting the approach I like to position myself about five metres underwater. This allows for some variation in depth, should the shark be submerging. Also, be mindful of the angle of the sun, so that you are using natural light to its full advantage.

Use of Strobes with Whale and Basking Sharks

Strobes are less useful for the following reasons:

- Plankton-rich water will increase backscatter problems.
- The extra drag will not help when bursts of speed are required.
- Strobe light will not give even coverage down the full length of the shark.
- For basking sharks, the use of strobe does not fit in with the recommended code of conduct.

In terms of safety, try and avoid positioning yourself directly in the path of the shark as it comes closer. You will be forcing it to change course and this constitutes harassment. Remember to keep well clear of the tail area. A blow from this could inflict damage ... on you.

Whale shark silhouette

Finally, choose your boat operator wisely. If they allow a full boat-load of snorkellers to descend on a single shark, then that is what you will come back with images of — plus or minus the shark, depending on your luck. You also want your boat crew keeping a careful eye on your safety with regard to other vessels in the area, getting in and out of the water and so on.

Codes of conduct for swimming with basking sharks can be found at www.sharktrust.org/en/basking_shark_resources

Manta Rays
by Anne-Marie Kitchen-Wheeler

These large members of the devil-ray family are a favourite of photographers due to the interaction between manta and photographer. My favourite photographs of mantas are those when the character of the animal is captured as well as some behaviour. Mantas have large brains and appear to be very curious of divers (freedivers or scuba divers) as long as a relationship is established. To

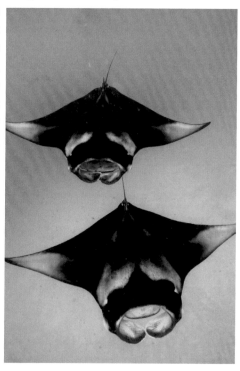

get the best out of a photographic session with mantas it is important to determine the behaviour of the subject because your approach will vary depending on this. Mantas are most likely to be encountered at cleaning stations (sites where they hover or make slow circles around colonies of cleaner fish — the species of which will vary depending where you are — and range from angelfish to very small cleaner wrasses) or when feeding.

At cleaning stations they tend to move more slowly and are best approached on scuba. When cleaning they are in their 'downtime' state and are easily disturbed, so I strongly advise not to freedive around mantas when they are being cleaned as they will be easily frightened and swim off. I propose that the manta sees the

Manta rays © Anne-Marie Kitchen Wheeler

diver as competing for the cleaning station and they do not understand our behaviour, feel threatened, and swim away. I encourage all divers to make eye contact with the manta before putting the camera eyepiece to your face. It really makes a difference. If you show no threat, they will continue their activity. All movements should be slow and deliberate and suggest no threat. If they swim away it may be because you have threatened them.

Feeding behaviour is very dynamic and is commonly a co-operative activity with many mantas interacting together, thus the presence of small groups of freedivers and snorkellers is well-tolerated. Mantas will often approach divers on the surface. The manta's eyes are located on the sides of its wide head, giving good peripheral vision, but poor vision directly in front of the animal. I suggest staying to the side of the manta so that it can see you and only making dives alongside so it can keep you in view. They move quickly when feeding so be prepared to swim with them to stay in contact, but stay horizontal when on the surface between dives.

As mantas are large use a wide-angled lens. Giant mantas grow to a wingspan of seven metres and even the smaller species commonly exceed wings spans of four metres. A 20mm lens is a good option if you are photographing a single subject but you will want a 10mm fisheye if there are a number of mantas present. It is not unusual for a manta to come closer than one metre to the photographer, providing an interesting portrait opportunity so the wider the better!

Unless you are night diving with them, they seem to tolerate strobes well and their dynamic movement demands a medium to fast shutter speed (1/100 sec or faster). Because they move around so much I sometimes use a semi-automatic mode on aperture priority to my desired colour of water and take a lot of shots. With most cameras you can select a mode which enables you to select shutter speed and/or aperture size: Tv, Av or P for both (check your camera manual as this varies). These settings allow the camera to make some of the choices for you to ensure the photograph is adequately exposed. A fairly fast shutter speed is required when shooting moving animals (1/100 sec or faster) and I select the aperture to give the colour of background water I prefer (take a test shot at the vista you expect the manta to be entering) and then allow the ISO to be in automatic to ensure an exposure. Use the flash to balance the shot when the manta comes into view. If the subject is moving around a great deal, and especially overhead, then setting aperture priority tends to reduce the number of overexposed shots compared to full manual. Alternately watch their movements and you can work out their swim patterns and then set the shot up for the best position.

Dr. Anne-Marie Kitchen-Wheeler works in the Maldives tourism and scuba travel industries. She monitors manta rays, having devised an individual identification method in order to conduct research on manta populations, movements and behaviours. She has contributed various articles on manta rays, sharks and diving medicine to nature, sport diving and travel magazines, dive travel and fish identification books and she enjoys making public presentations about manta rays and sharks. She is also a keen underwater photographer and five times UK Ladies Champion Freediver.

Jellyfish

Unlike some of the aforementioned creatures, jellyfish are not difficult to photograph, and the results can be quite stunning. Many land-based photographers are able to obtain good results shooting through glass aquariums, so as an underwater photographer you have the opportunity to do much better.

I have a fairly simple process which works well for me. Firstly, I dispense with my strobes. Jellyfish make use of a biofluorescent property that makes them appear self-illuminated, with just a few rays of sunlight. Strobing them *can* lose this effect and make the image look rather flat.

Secondly, I tend to pick out subjects that are three or four metres below the surface. Just deep enough to darken the background, but without losing too much of the ambient light highlighting the jelly. For the same reason I prefer to shoot in deep water, so that there is no sandy bottom reflecting light back up and providing a distracting background.

I find a wide-angle lens to be a more flexible choice as it can be moved forward to capture close-up detail, or pulled back to reveal the full extent of trailing filaments. If I were specifically looking for smaller creatures (or knew that these were the only size to be expected) then macro would be the alternate lens choice. Some jellyfish are the size of a fingernail.

Perspectives

Cyanea lamarckii — bluefire jellyfish

This approach is my own preference; I am aware though that other photographers favour alternate methods and have amazing images to back that up. There is a good guide at www.uwphotography-guide.com/jellyfish-salps-pelagic-inverts and not all of it fits my own recipe. I give you my suggestion but you should experiment with others.

Regarding jellyfish and their stings, these creatures can be deceiving. Some of the more threatening looking may have little or no sting, and some fairly benign-looking ones can deliver quite painful stings. Having been at the receiving end of the latter, I now cover up with a full hooded wetsuit and gloves when jellyfish are around. Bad stings can cause discomfort for weeks after the event. As with other creatures you photograph, a little research beforehand can be a wise investment of your time.

Sea Birds, Reptiles and Amphibians

Images of birds such as guillemots and cormorants feeding are becoming more popular. For the sake of some amusement, I have included here an effort of my own which has the potential for much improvement. Birds that dive beneath the surface and effectively fly through the water provide a striking and dynamic image. In general, they tend to be less concerned about human presence than those resting on the surface. It is interesting to note that puffins (when nesting) allow reasonably close contact with humans, but are a lot less tolerant when floating in the water. They can be quite skittish and view us as more of a threat in that environment. There's an evaluation to be made between the aesthetic appeal of a floating bird's nether regions versus the difficulty of the approach.

The most common underwater reptile you are likely to encounter will be one of the species of sea turtle. A frequently captured image is one taken while

Glass and Water

positioned in their path of travel, just as they veer off to avoid making contact. The lens choice here being wide-angle to improve the opportunity of a sun-burst and/or another diver. A lens that provides coverage of one hundred degrees or more would allow a turtle and other compositional elements to fit within a single frame.

However, if you are at or near the surface and have a turtle directly below, then you can get good results with the shell pattern when using

An inquisitive cormorant — just being nosey!

available light. For this sort of shot, shoot in raw and experiment with white balance settings in post-processing, to balance the shell tones with the blue background. I'd only really attempt the image capture at a distance of no more than a couple of metres. Larger turtles make good silhouettes when positioned between the lens and the sun, and countless other close-ups due to their tolerance of our presence underwater.

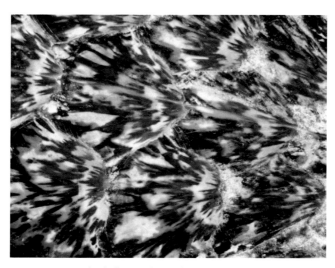

Turtle shells can also make interesting abstract images

Large reptiles — saltwater crocodiles for example — are perhaps better left for photographing from a safe distance … or using a pole camera from a boat, **but take local guidance**. A pole camera is operated remotely at the end of a pole or bar. It is useful in situations where it is not safe for the photographer to be in the water. There are exceptions to this where some crocodiles are approachable in the water, but you'll want some concrete assurances when and where this is the case.

One of the most surreal scenes I have witnessed was a shoal of thousands upon thousands of tadpoles surrounding a submerged boat in a lake. I had no camera with me that day, so cannot prove the claim, but something I won't forget in a hurry. We're more used to seeing the activity of the frogs that bring about the tadpoles! I have also seen some excellent 'split-level' images with a frog as the subject, and intend to attempt one of these shots in the future.

Homo Delphinus, aka the Aquatic Ape

The late, great freediver Jacques Mayol devised the term *Homo Delphinus* to classify a species he otherwise referred to as the Aquatic Ape. This was an (unproven) ancestor of mankind that had a similar physical appearance and lived in the ocean. It is a romantic notion for freedivers, and appears to explain some of our aquatic adaptations such as the mammalian reflex.

This section of the chapter is devoted to photographing people underwater (after all, are we not creatures?). Freedivers are by and large willing subjects, but finding an opportunity can be a challenge, certainly with those who compete. Freediving competitions are actually a bit of a closed affair. Opening and closing ceremonies tend to be fairly public, but the events themselves normally have limited spaces for photographers, and these are usually professionals who are experienced in capturing the images without compromising safety procedures. Competitive freedivers do of course train, and two of the principle depth training locations both go by the same name — 'The Blue Hole'. One is found just north of Dahab in the Sinai Peninsula, Egypt, and the other on Long Island in the Bahamas. In the UK, open water training takes place in some of the deeper flooded quarries. Visibility and water temperature favour the Bahamian and Egyptian locations!

Needless to say, you will need to obtain permission from individuals you wish to photograph, and this should be made some time in advance. If you see

Glass and Water

A capture angle of upward forty-five degrees can produce good results

a freediver near to a float/line assembly, the more relaxed they look, the less likely they will want to be interrupted. Chances are they will be focusing and preparing for a dive.

As a freediving photographer you are far more likely to receive a favourable response from a competitive freediver to a photography request than a scuba diving photographer would. You may think this to be related to your common interest in freediving, but in fact there are more practical reasons. Firstly, the bubble factor — it isn't just fish that don't like bubbles; a lot of freedivers loathe having to swim through them. This may be something you come to sympathise with. The other aspect is lack of visibility. Competitive freedivers focus on the guide line in front of them, not the direction they are swimming in. Scuba divers have a degree of hard metal around them and may not have the experience to leave enough room (especially for the monofinner, who will snake toward and away from the line). I have witnessed near-accidents where recreational scuba divers have taken the liberty of using a freediving guide line on which to perform safety stops. They are usually faced with the prospect of enraged freedivers at the surface!

As a freediver photographing competitive freedivers, as well as asking permission you need to give plenty of room and steer well clear of any descent line. You also need to be aware of surrounding safety divers. A surfacing competitive freediver is always accompanied by a safety freediver.

From a photographic viewpoint, if you have an extremely wide-angle lens fitted, then you may not be able to approach closely enough to fill the frame with the diver. Also, if you are photographing an ascent you may well have more than one person in the frame. If your lens of choice here is wide-angle zoom, then you have that extra flexibility not present with the use of a prime lens.

Shots that work well are often taken at a depth lower than the subject, and at an angle of forty-five degrees. If you are capturing a descent, then a strobe is normally needed to light the subject's face (if they are happy for you to strobe). The ascent normally works well with natural light, especially if you can perfect the angle necessary for sunlight to reflect from the mask.

If you are able to use Snell's window as well, then so much the better. Shallow, and in calm waters, whatever is above the surface can be seen through a circular 'window' created by an approximately one hundred degree cone, outside of which a reflection is seen instead.

Images captured from above the subject will maximise ambient light, but you also need to consider the closing speed of the person who is ascending.

 Whether you are photographing freedivers, swimmers or hair-clips; **do not expect to be able to turn up at your local swimming pool** with camera and housing in tow. Most do not allow photography when the general public are

Glass and Water

present. Some pools are less stringent when a private hire has been arranged, but you'll usually still need permission from both the hirer and pool management.

Underwater videographer turned model

If you are able to obtain permission or have the use of a private swimming pool, then there are many photographic opportunities to be found. Swimmers and babies are good subjects, as are staged artistic compositions with models. The bonus of using a swimming pool is that temperature and water clarity are often favourable.

Aside from freedivers and people in swimming pools, there is still plenty of human subject matter in our rivers, lakes and oceans. Scuba divers are obvious candidates, although you may feel you have enough images of those if you are a scuba diver yourself. Surfers are an interesting challenge, as you are likely to have two subjects: the rolling surf and the person with the board. Other possibilities are pearl divers, spear fishers, canoeists practising rolls, or even boat owners giving their hulls a scrub. Wherever there is a stretch of water there's usually an excuse for someone to get wet!

The obvious benefit with photographing people is that they can co-operate, and be part of a staged composition. Drawing on my experience as a freediver having to occasionally sign media disclaimer forms, I now always take the precaution of asking permission before pressing the shutter.

Others

I have tried in this chapter to provide a mixture of subjects that I and others have either experienced attempting to gain images of, or believe would make interesting subjects. The list could go on and is by no means complete. Our world's watery domain has dugongs, sailfish, sardine shoals and countless other species. Mankind is endangering the survival of some of these animals, and they may not be there forever. Images of endangered species help bring attention to their plight, so **what you capture on your sensor could be more important than you realise**.

Perspectives

Hunting sailfish © Danny Kessler

Glass and Water

Radio Tags

You may find some larger sea creatures with radio tags fitted. This means that their movements and behaviour are of interest to someone somewhere, and that this is likely to be for the benefit of the animal. So your observations and photographs may aid that cause if you seek out the organisation concerned after the interaction.

Female Tiger shark with radio tag attached to dorsal fin.

A physical description of the tag may prove useful, as well as unusual features and markings on the creature (bite marks, notches on fins, missing parts, etc.). Never attempt to remove a radio tag.

Summary

Here are some key points for each species covered in the chapter:

- Manatees — do not disturb those feeding/resting, do not initiate physical contact.
- Sea lions/seals — be prepared for rapid movement and use a robust pair of fins!
- Dolphins — keep them entertained, but retreat if they become too familiar.
- Pilot whales — keep your distance and treat with caution and respect.
- Sharks — be constantly vigilant about changes in behaviour.
- Basking/whale sharks — intercept their path of travel; consider silhouettes.
- Manta rays — make eye contact before introducing the camera.
- Sea birds, amphibians, etc. — niche subjects, an opportunity for an original image.
- People — for staged subjects you can prepare and plan ahead.

Blue jellyfish rising
[Panasonic GF1 with 7–14mm lens,
INON housing, f8 at 1/100s, ISO 400]

A Virtual Dive

'You cannot depend on your eyes when your imagination is out of focus'
Mark Twain[1]

The Mission

The Sea of the Hebrides: part of the North Atlantic Ocean located off the coast of western Scotland, separating the mainland and the northern Inner Hebrides islands (to the east) from the southern Outer Hebrides islands (to the west). It is July, and marine wildlife is in abundance at this time of year — everything from congregating basking sharks to minke whales and nesting puffins. Your photographic mission, however, is something quite different. There have been reports of the Oceanic sunfish (or Mola mola) in the area, which are not typically found here. You intend to record their presence as a series of underwater digital stills images for a project you are working on.

Aboard a rigid inflatable boat (RIB) heading out of Tobermory on the Isle of Mull, you have chosen to photograph with a medium form camera plus wide-angle lens and no strobes, in order to maximise your manoeuvrability in the water. Sunfish can move with surprising speed. Typically you would aim to shoot them from just under the surface, but you have the training and experience to go deeper if need be.

There are four of you in total: the boat skipper, wildlife spotter, your dive partner and you. Seas are thankfully flat-calm, but with barely a breath of wind and the sun out in full force. You decide to leave donning your wetsuit until a little closer to the intended dive area. The sunfish have been sighted previously some three miles to the west of the Isle of Coll, the water will be deep there. You have your SOUPA float (see *Chapter 7: Descents and Ascents*), which although you doubt you'll need for deploying your camera will still serve a useful purpose for support. The attached diver's flag and guide line are also of great benefit.

---

1   *A Connecticut Yankee in King Arthur's Court* (1889) USA: Charles L Webster and Co.

Perspectives

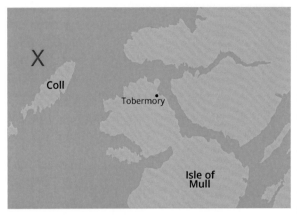

X marks the spot

As the RIB skims across the glassy surface, you visualise the task ahead. The sun angle, colour of the water, and flatness of the ocean will all have a bearing on both the camera settings and the type of image you want to portray. Will there be an opportunity for a silhouette or 'split-level' type image, or do you want to focus on creative underwater surface reflections?

You may capture an image of a basking shark

Gearing Up

The wetsuit you will wear today is tailor made for you, a two-piece hooded suit made from 5mm smoothskin Heiwa neoprene. It is time to prepare it for wearing, so you coat the insides liberally with some lubricant. In just a couple of minutes you have both sections on, as well as your neoprene socks.

Next on is your Marseillaise weight belt and low profile lead weights. You make sure it sits low down on your hips so that your abdomen has enough room for efficient deep breathing. This is swiftly followed by your dive computer on your left wrist and your neoprene wrist strap with D-ring on your right. The D-ring will later secure your camera assembly via a lanyard.

No sunfish have yet been spotted, and after ten or fifteen minutes, you rather feel that suiting up may have been a little premature. You are gradually warming, and in another ten to fifteen minutes it will start to become uncomfortable. You gulp a few mouthfuls of water from your bottle and then, suddenly, the ideal solution presents itself.

You have noticed that there are a number of large lion's mane jellyfish in the water and, as the sunfish have not yet appeared, these would make for good photographic subjects. The added benefit would be some cooling down.

The skipper cuts the engines and you and your partner complete the kitting-up process. Your low-volume mask is prepared for defogging, and you are careful to avoid trapping either your hair or wetsuit hood as you put it onto your face. This is easier to do with un-gloved fingers; the 3mm gloves go on afterward. Last on are your carbon fibre fins, which are probably the most difficult item to squeeze into. You want the pockets to be tight but not uncomfortable, so that you maximise the transfer of power from foot to fin.

Submergence

Your partner has helpfully set up the SOUPA float, so that when you slip into the water alongside it you can put both snorkel and camera inside the main tube. You have previously dip-tested the camera to check that no bubbles emerge from the casing. The guide line leads fifteen metres down to the weights.

Stowing camera following dip test

The pair of you now push yourselves and the float away from the boat. You retrieve your camera, attach the lanyard to your wrist strap and switch it on. The battery is on full power, the SD card has no images recorded, and all settings are as expected. Now is the right time for a depth check.

First though, you take a good couple of minutes to breathe. Face down in the water with your snorkel in place, every breath you take is slow and extends both down into your abdomen as well as the upper lung lobes. A feeling of wellbeing ensues as you watch the shafts of sunlight dancing their way into the deep.

For your last breath, the water is calm enough for you to remove your snorkel and breathe in with your head up and out of the water. You are also able to make a pre-dive equalisation. With your camera in one hand, you use the other to pull the guide line toward you. As you do so, the combined weight of the ballast on the line and that you are carrying (both camera and weight belt) draws you beneath the surface. You discover that you are equalising underwater success-fully, so the first check box of your mental list can be ticked (see *Chapter 7: Descents and Ascents*).

The eight metre stop

You intend to continue your descent using your arm, thereby conserving your leg muscles. As you pull deeper you start to pause now and again to look at the line. This gives you an idea of where you are with your buoyancy. Eventually you check your dive computer and you realise that you have reached neutral buoyancy. It reads eight metres.

Visibility is good today. In fact it is sensational for these parts — at least fifteen metres — and this means your partner at the surface is able to monitor you visually. As you look around, there are one or two blue jellyfish nearby, and at the edge of visibility what appears to be a lion's mane can just be seen. You will have ample opportunity to find another later, so for now you take a test shot of a nearby blue jellyfish. The image on the LCD display looks acceptable, but viewing the display underwater can be decep-tive so you check the histogram. You can see curves edging to the right, and in fact the image is a little overexposed. You want the subject to stand out against

Perspectives

the background, and therefore increase the shutter speed by one increment. Another test shot and you are now happy with your camera settings.

After roughly a minute, the urge to breathe is just starting to make its presence felt. This is the signal to surface, and slowly but deliberately you pull yourself back to the fresh air. As you break the surface, you flop both arms over the SOUPA float and simultaneously gulp in a good lungful of air. You face your partner so that she can clearly see your eyes, as you smile and tell her, 'I'm OK!'

The test shot through a 7–14mm lens, f8 at 1/100s, ISO 400. No strobe.

Your partner now needs to do her weight and camera checks, so you keep your face down in the water to watch while breathing deeply through your snorkel. She also takes just over a minute, so while she is recovering from her own breath-hold, you both discuss the dives ahead and your strategy.

The Shoot

You could surface swim with the float to the nearest lion's mane jellyfish, and position yourselves above it. This may create a few issues though. Firstly, you know that a surface swim will use more

Partner takes her turn

energy than an underwater one. Secondly, the guide line may be visible in the image. Thirdly, the float may cast a shadow over the subject. So no, you will leave the float where it is, and locate the subject by finning horizontally from your neutral depth.

Perspectives

You and your partner have now been at the surface for five and three minutes respectively. The previous breath-holds mean that your bodies are conditioned to expect a further increase of carbon dioxide, and your haemoglobin has now re-bonded to the oxygen it surrendered earlier. You will dive first.

Your preparation is the same as before but this time, after ditching your snorkel, you crease your abdomen and lower your upper body down into the water. Simultaneously, your legs rise up in the air and the weight of them serves to push most of your body downwards. With your free arm you make an outward scoop to propel you further, so that your fin tips slip beneath the surface without so much as a ripple.

Almost ready for the duck dive — the mass of the legs will propel you downward once above your hips

There are five movements to now synchronise in one go (but you have practised these many times before at your local freediving club's pool sessions):

1. Your hand moves up to your nose for your first submerged equalisation.

2. The elbow of the arm you have just moved, you tuck in close to your body to improve hydrodynamic efficiency.

3. You tuck in your chin for the same reason, and to ease equalisations.

4. The hand carrying your camera is moved down alongside your hip (your medium form camera is small enough to allow this; a large form camera or rig with strobe would have meant raising your arm to provide the water-break).

5. Lastly, you deliver two or three forceful kicks, but without a wide separation of your legs. You are on your way down.

As you descend, you watch the guide line and ensure it is passing you parallel to your body. You avoid the temptation to look down; this would mean losing sight of the line and your arching neck would impair the slipstream. The accelerating speed of the moving guide line tells you that you can ease your fin kicks. Within a few seconds, your depth alarm warns you that you have reached seven metres. By the time you have reacted and grabbed the guide line to halt your descent, another metre has been added.

Attaining a horizontal position, you make a visual radial search around you. Some twelve metres away and a couple of metres shallower, a lion's mane is clearly visible. The surrounding water is somewhat lighter and bluer than your previous position, so results should be good.

The challenge is now on. Ascending level to the jellyfish will make you positively buoyant, which means that as you compose and focus you will be moving upwards and away. Also, to maximise your hydrodynamic profile, you want to swim horizontally at precisely the depth where you are located. This presents a slight issue, in that maintaining a visual reference could prove tricky.

You certainly do not want to arch your neck backwards. But you can tilt your head up a little, and roll your eyes upwards to look through the very top of your mask. This won't spoil your profile too much.

Your profile is similar to that on your descent, but now with your body perpendicular to the previous line of travel. Also, the hand and arm you use to equalise is alongside your body. Fin kicks are deliberate, but at about fifty percent of maximum thrust. Your legs rise and fall with a measured separation; definitely not with deep or wide kicks.

As you move, you know where your subject is and you can see the exact angle of the sun from the direction of the sun's rays below you. You have time to think about where you want to be positioned so that the sun is behind you and lighting your subject.

You have reached the point where the jellyfish would be at the correct focusing distance if it were level. Now you need to ascend. As you do so, you are looking through the LCD and the jellyfish starts to fill the frame, so you compose the subject. You are still below, and making a judgement on the correct angle at which to fire the shot. Although now slightly positively buoyant, you slow down your ascent by flaring out your legs and fins. This also helps to stabilise you. The opportunity presents itself, and you depress the shutter.

Perspectives

Mission #1 accomplished

Now you have a choice. You could bracket the image with further captures using exposure compensation, or trust your judgement and ascend. You choose the latter.

Surfacing

Fin kicks to the surface are paced and regular — no need to rush. Your free hand is above you, and you glance up to see your partner overhead. Although she wasn't able to keep up with you during your distance swim, she caught up while you were taking the photograph. She has helpfully brought the float closer, but not so much so that it would interfere with your photography.

Your free hand and arm break the surface, and as your head follows you exhale fully and inhale. The float is two or three metres away; you need to fin sufficiently to keep your head above water and move toward it. Your recovery breathing continues as you fin. Only when you have reached it and are fully supported, do you give your partner the OK message.

A humming noise in the background has been a little distracting, but now it is diminishing. This is fortunately not a symptom of hypoxia, but a four-rotor drone that the boat crew have sent up to film from the air. The drone will help them locate fish they cannot otherwise see from the boat. Your partner is ready now for her dive, but just as she prepares to go, there is a cry from the boat twenty metres away: 'Mola mola, Mola mola!!'.

Neptune reflecting

[Panasonic GF1 with 7–14mm lens, INON housing, f8 at 1/100s, ISO 400]

Facing Reality

If we base our imagination on a thread of reality, then I believe it brings the vision to life. 'A Virtual Dive' was borne out of such reality. In the summer of 2014, some of the events visualised took place in the described location. There were a few more on board the boat than the four described, and the objective then was to photograph basking sharks. However the seas were flat calm, the sun was out in force, and we really did see the pictured Mola mola in clear blue water.

In the next chapter we take this a step further and hear from three freediving underwater photographers.

Basking shark
© Shane Wasik / Basking Shark Scotland

Behind the Lens

'Sometimes when we are generous in small, barely detectable ways it can change someone else's life forever'

Margaret Cho

Various contributors to this book have kindly supplied photographs, articles and in one case an entire underwater experience to draw upon (*Chapter 12: A Virtual Dive*). We have much to learn from these talented people, and in this chapter I have asked three of them to share their passion and experiences of freediving underwater photography. They echo many of the ideas put forward in the book, but there is still much to learn from their varied approaches.

Interview with Shane Wasik

Shane, could you please tell us a little about the photographic equipment you use while freediving and why you have chosen that configuration?

I have used Nikon SLRs in Aquatica housings since 2009 and prior to that with Sea&Sea housings, even going back to the Motormarine and Nikonos Vs in the early days! My current preferred rig is the Nikon D7100 and Tokina 10–17mm lens, coupled with either a four or eight inch dome port. This setup gives excellent quality whilst not breaking the bank. The Aquatica housings are rugged enough for professional use and the setup works well for a range of big animals which I focus on these days. When freediving it tends to be all ambient light for streamlining, leaving the strobes for when I'm using scuba. However I still use the versatile GoPros, sometimes attached to the top of the housing or separately on a little handle, they are great for shooting video and capture great footage!

Are there any problems or obstacles you have had to overcome while freediving with your camera?

Unlike scuba, you don't have many places to attach a large camera to if you're relaxing on the surface, or waiting for the boat pickup. I like to have a D-ring attached to my weight belt so I can clip my camera off and I know it is secure! Especially in the open ocean, where there is no visible bottom. Our primary operations are in the Hebrides where most divers would wear drysuits, however we've found that modern wetsuits are still warm and have little drag for freediving. I currently use a 5mm surf wetsuit which has excellent flexibility and minimal flushing (the real key to keeping warm). As such you only need a small weight belt.

Would you mind sharing with us any hints or tips that have helped with your freediving photography?
Good preparation for the dive is essential in capturing good images. If you dive with bad technique or inefficient breathing you're starting off badly. It is also good practice to visualise the image you wish to take before the dive, you might wish to dive a spot a couple of times to work out your angle of approach, composition and settings. Then relax and take some time to prepare for the dive and then shoot a great image! However this advice only works for reef scenes. Anything that's moving and particularly big animals, then you need to pre-set everything before you get off the boat. I've seen a lot of people wait till they get the 'Go, go, go!' signal to fiddle about with their camera settings, missing the opportunity they travelled all the way to see in the first place. Once you are in the water with big animals then there is a whole other set of rules to consider. Sometimes photographers get a bad reputation for not respecting their subject and this is as true in the ocean as it is on land. Study the animals beforehand, earn their trust, use good technique, shoot a great image and leave no trace!

Could you let us know more about your scuba and freediving background please?
I learned to freedive in my early teens on holidays and around the local coastline, so by the time I was able to start scuba at sixteen I was already very comfortable in the water. Freediving in the ocean isn't always about being able to hold your breath, it is about having watermanship skills too, reading the waves, currents, topography — it is a dynamic environment! Also important is having good all-round fitness for operating in that kind of environment. If you're not comfortable in the water then you're not going to get good images.

How have you developed your skillset?

I've taken up yoga recently, which is great for increasing your core strength, along with mastering breathing techniques and focus. As we have a number of freedivers coming on our trips, then we get exposed to various techniques which we can use to help us with our own. We have also become an Undersea Soft Encounter Alliance (USEA) centre, under the teaching of Pierre Robert de Latour. This is all about interaction with marine mammals and the freediving techniques to enable close interaction with zero impact.

What proportion of images do you capture while freediving?

With Basking Shark Scotland our wildlife tours in the Hebrides, it is all about the megafauna. The techniques that we have developed are all based on freediving as scuba just doesn't work with all the faff, noise and gear. So all of our images are now mainly captured via freediving. Trips to the seal colonies, island reefs, Fingals cave and even shallow shipwrecks can all be freedived; although we still scuba dive on the deeper reefs and the bigger wrecks.

Shane, thank you very much.

Shane Wasik is owner of Basking Shark Scotland, a wildlife and diving company based in the Hebrides, which organises summer expeditions to find the gentle giants of the Atlantic. He is a qualified marine biologist, along with being a published underwater photographer and highly qualified diver. He started freediving as a teenager and leaned scuba at sixteen, then picked up his first underwater camera during his commercial diving course in 2001.

Danny Kessler

I specialise in shooting megafauna and for nearly all of these subjects, snorkelling or freediving is the only practical way to work. I tend to freedive with large subjects, such as whales, which are very hard to get close to with scuba. The additional manoeuvrability one has as a freediver makes all the difference between success and failure. Most of my best images have been taken just under the surface, where scuba offers only disadvantages.

I use Nikon D700 and D800 camera bodies, preferring full frame sensor for the image quality it yields when enlarged. When providing images for the Tethys Megafauna Exhibition,[1] my largest print, of a blue whale, was 1.5 metres wide. I use Subal housings. I usually equip one body with a 16mm fisheye lens for very large subjects, like fin whales, or for getting close to easily approached animals like manatees. I also use the 16mm for shooting split-levels. I use the Nikon 17–35mm wide-angle zoom for more evasive or smaller subjects and for portraits of large animals, when the 16mm fisheye is too wide. I rarely use flash, and especially like the Nikons for their lack of noise at high ISOs. When available light is poor because it is overcast and you need high shutter speeds to freeze the action, and medium apertures for sharpness, you are forced to use high ISOs. On an exhibition size print, with a green or blue ocean background, noise becomes very obvious.

Danny Kessler is a world class underwater adventure photographer specialising in marine megafauna who has exhibited his images at a number of prestigious festivals and been published widely. Exploring the world's seas and oceans, Danny's work is recognised for not only its intimate style but also for the unique experiences he captures. Danny aims to raise awareness to promote protection of the critically endangered species he is privileged to encounter.

---

1   See www.tethys.org

Blue whale © Danny Kessler

When I do use flash, I use paired INON Z-240 strobes. They are small, which minimises drag. They also recycle extremely quickly. This is essential when burst shooting feeding sailfish, for example. Occasionally I'll trade off using full frame and switch to APS-C (see *Glossary*) and use the Tokina 10–17 zoom. I can then use higher flash sync speeds, helping to put a sparkle into the subject's eyes or darken the background for contrast, while still freezing the movement of a speeding animal.

When freediving, the subjects are often curious about you rather than spooked as when you use scuba. Some animals love their reflection in the dome and this attracts them, but others seem to see the dome as a big aggressive eye they would rather avoid. I often keep my dome facing down so as not to cause a reaction unless I am sure it will be curiosity, rather than aggression.

Aggression indicates you've stressed your subject, which we should try hard to avoid. Curiosity can lead to a wonderful, sustained encounter and your pictures will be all the better for it.

I always try to maintain a mental compass as to where the sun is and keep it on my back or on my side but never want to shoot subjects coming from the direction of the sun. All the particulate shows up in the water, it is unforgiving and unflattering. People associate backscatter with using flash, but it is frequently there in the plankton rich water in which many big animals are feeding — often the only situation in which they can be photographed successfully.

Laura Storm

My first experience of underwater imaging was handling an Amphibico video housing whilst filming competitive freedivers in the cold depths of Canadian waters. Many years later, I never could have anticipated that I would embrace freediving principles to the degree that I have. The differences between technical diving and freediving are profound enough but, when you factor photography into the equation, the contrasts become even more evident.

The transition from equipment intensive technical diving to a more alpinist approach has been both refreshing and something of a revelation. The right hydrodynamic gear, long-bladed fins and a custom-made Heiwa suit have collectively helped to advance my photography. I'm obviously able to move faster, get in closer to the peak-of-action and have valuable extra seconds when it matters. A distinct advantage is that I can be more 'in the moment' with what I'm doing, since I'm less distracted by gadgets, time limitations and decompression obligations, among other considerations.

As a result, almost half of my winning and published images have been taken when freediving. I've been able to experiment more shooting with natural light and have enjoyed incredible up-close wildlife interaction. In part, that's because I've deliberately sought destinations or subjects that lend themselves to freediving, like the Scottish Hebrides, remote rivers and places with tricky shore entries. In turn, my portfolio has benefited from the added variety this has brought.

My camera of choice is a Canon SLR in a Sea & Sea housing. I particularly like the weight and size of my rig. It just feels right in my hands, like it belongs. I spent months researching underwater camera options as I wanted something that would suit all terrains and all types of diving. I've ended up with a combination that has substance and responds fast when I'm expecting it to, allows me to shoot manual, capture raw, high resolution images and delivers the quality I'm after. I can switch easily between stills and video and the quick access feature enables me to change settings on the fly when the heat is on.

Winner of British Society of Underwater Photographers 'Focus On'
Competition, May 2014 © Laura Storm/Planet Plankton

Typically, I prefer to freedive without strobes and use ambient light instead. If I'm shooting wide-angle, I'll almost always opt to use my 15mm fisheye lens and a compact dome port to streamline as much as possible. For the times when I decide to add strobes, I try to visualise first what I'm after. That allows me to work out ahead of time the settings and rough angles. Then I tuck the strobe arms tight in towards the housing until I'm more or less where I need to be in the water. At the last moment, I pull the arms up to where I want them and shoot away.

One-on-one instruction has helped me tackle the issues I've had with head-down equalisation. I'm prone to sticky ears and so I've learnt to equalise earlier and more often when I'm freediving than I need to when on scuba. I've also adopted a conditioning, pre-dive equalisation before I leave the surface.

Perhaps the most useful lesson for me has been in regard to my weighting. It makes all the difference in the world being able to hold a depth while composing an image. So the time I spend working out and positioning my weights in relation to the suit I'm using, the weight of my rig and the depth where I'll be neutrally buoyant more than pays its dues.

It is an immense privilege to spend time in the oceans with so many unique animals. Everything about this special realm is unpredictable, challenging and at times deeply frustrating. You need to be opportunistic and adaptable if you are to maximise the chances that come your way. Timing is paramount, especially when it comes to capturing behaviour and peak-of-action images. Knowing your subject, its habitat, patterns of movement, its likes and dislikes — gives you an advantage in recognising when that moment is right; when a scene is playing out in front of you and the magic starts to come together.

And of course, there's always that element of luck!

Laura Storm is a passionate and accomplished wildlife photographer. She is a Trimix diver and led the Angels Technical Dive Team through seven years of challenges, supporting a number of major International and National Freediving events before disbanding in 2010. She was named 'Buddy of the Year' by *Diver Magazine* in 2006 for her contribution as a support diver.

In 2010 she set up Planet Plankton, committed to advancing marine conservation and raising awareness for the oceans through photography and photo journalism. More recently she has been invited to collaborate with the Sylvia Earle Alliance and their Mission Blue project. She is involved in supporting Google Earth's 'Ocean Layer' as an 'Explorer of the Oceans Story Contributor'.

She has acted as technical consultant for the diving scenes in Simon Mayo's children's adventure book series and occasionally writes poetry and diving related articles.

Her winning images can be found at www.planetplankton.co.uk

SHARK!

Baby there's a shark in the bathroom
A sharp shooter in a silver suit
Shapeshifting in the shadows
Blue and Evil on his mind.

Baby there's a shark on the ceiling
A debt collector with a bottle-opening tail
Smudging nature's paint work
Soup stain on his soul.

Baby there's a shark in the mirror
A '63 roadster on the prowl
Cryptic grey striped camouflage
Guarded question in his eyes.

Baby there's a shark in the water
A trigger-happy revolutionary
Swimming against a crimson tide
Pelagic Tiger by my side.

Laura Storm

Glossary

Italicised words are *cross-references* to items in the glossary (or *foreign words*).

Aerobic (exercise)	Exercise involving the use of oxygen to supply energy demands.
AIDA International	*Association Internationale pour le Développement de l'Apnée.* International Association for Development of Apnea. Worldwide freediving organisation.
Anaerobic (exercise)	Exercise involving the use of internal fuels other than oxygen to supply energy demands.
Antioxidant	A molecule that inhibits oxidation of other molecules. Helps the body prevent the damaging effects of oxidation from *Free radicals*.
Aperture	Adjustable opening to allow light to pass through a lens. The adjustment governs the quantity of light passing through and therefore affects overall exposure.
Apnea	A word of Greek derivation that means the suspension of breathing.
APS-C	Advanced Photo System type-C. An image sensor format used by the majority of *DSLR* systems not employing the larger 'full frame' format. Also referred to as 'cropped frame', this format is increasingly being used by mirrorless systems.
Backscatter	Illumination of tiny particles in the water that bounce *Strobe* light back through the camera lens. This appears as a snow-like interference.
Bends, The	See *Decompression sickness (DCS)*.
BFA	The British Freediving Association, a volunteer-managed UK freediving organisation.
Blackout	Full loss of consciousness.
Bottom time	Time spent at depth where the freediver neither ascends nor further descends.
Bracketing	The capture of multiple images with differing variables, the most typical of these being the level of exposure.

Bradycardia	A resting heart rate of less than 60 beats per minute.
Breathing-up	Deep breathing combined with inner mental focus in the stages approaching a freedive.
BSoUP	The British Society of Underwater Photographers — the largest underwater photographic society in Britain.
Cleaning station	An underwater formation where small marine creatures congregate for the purposes of removing parasites and superficial debris from larger creatures.
Composition	The organisation of visual elements according to artistic principles.
Cyanosis	Blue or purple skin colouration due to low oxygen saturation.
Decompression sickness (DCS)	Also known as 'the bends'. A condition that arises from gases dissolved within bodily fluids and tissues that emerge from solution as bubbles.
Denticles	Tooth-like scales found on the outer layer of cartilaginous fishes such as sharks and rays.
Drag coefficient	A calculable quantity to define the resistance of an object in a fluid environment such as air or water.
DSLR/SLR	Camera using a mirror and prism for the photographer to view directly through the lens to see what will be captured. DSLR stands for Digital Single-Lens Reflex, and SLR for Single-Lens Reflex (film only).
Duck dive	Submersion method brought about by bringing the legs upward and perpendicular to the water's surface, thereby pushing the upper part of the body below the water line.
Dynamic apnea	Competitive freediving discipline that involves swimming submerged and parallel to the surface.
Equalisation	In diving terms, a reference to balancing pressure between two compartments that are adjacent to each other, where at least one of the compartments is gaseous, for example mask and sinuses.
Eustachian tube	Tube that provides a link between the middle ear and nasopharynx.
F-stop	A numerical value prefixed with 'f' that is the ratio of the lens focal length to its *Aperture*'s diameter. The larger the number the smaller the aperture. The smaller the aperture the larger the depth of field (and vice versa)

Freediving Actualisation Triangle (FAT)	Formed from the three components of equipment, technique and training.
Fin amplitude	The distance between the furthest point of the upward kick on one leg and the lowest point of the downward kick on the other.
Fin slippage	A sideways twisting of the fin so that it slices through the water instead of pushing against it.
Fixed lens	A lens that is fixed to the camera body and part of the overall construction. Not to be confused with a fixed focal length lens (see *Prime lens*).
Form systems	A categorisation of camera systems used solely within this publication, that positions camera equipment into one of four forms: small, medium, large or oversize.
Free radicals	Atoms or groups of atoms with an odd (unpaired) number of electrons, which can damage cells in the human body. Intense exercise and breath-holding are thought to be contributing factors to their generation, among many others.
Freedivers Recovery Vest	FRV: A jacket that automatically inflates after a pre-programmed depth or time limit has been exceeded.
Full frame sensor	A sensor size which approximates 35mm standard film frames, measuring 36×24mm.
Gauge mode, computer	A dive computer option that provides depth and dive duration information, but which excludes decompression monitoring.
Guide line	A vertical line leading directly downward from the surface, typically tied off with lead weight at the bottom end. Can also be referred to as a 'shot' or 'descent' line.
Haemoglobin	A blood protein that acts as a transport mechanism for oxygen transferring between the lungs and the rest of the body.
Heat run, whale	Aggressive behaviour between rival males of the same whale species, whereby they jostle for mating rights with the females.

Histogram	Graphical representation of the distribution of data. On camera LCDs, this represents pixels with different values and can be used to determine if an image is under or over-exposed.
Housing	A waterproof case for the containment of a camera. Usually with *Ports*.
Hyperventilation	Rapid and shallow breathing that causes the lowering of carbon dioxide in blood plasma. It is a causative factor of *Shallow water blackout*.
Hypothermia	Lowering of the body's core temperature to the point where metabolic processes can no longer function satisfactorily.
Hypoxia	A condition where the body experiences inadequate oxygen saturation.
Hypoxic event	A manifestation of *Hypoxia* where an abnormal situation or behaviour takes place. This can range between poor responsiveness to full unconsciousness (*Blackout*).
Interchangeable lens	A lens which detaches from the camera body, usually via a bayonet or screw mount mechanism or *Port*.
ISO	Measure of light sensitivity. The higher the number, the more sensitive the sensor will be to light. In digital cameras this can be varied (in film cameras it remained constant for the roll being used). Along with *Aperture* and *Shutter speed*, this will govern the degree of exposure.
Lactic acid	A weak, organic acid that partially dissociates in water producing ion lactate. It is a substance generated from the *Anaerobic* breakdown of glycogen to effect energy in muscles when oxygen levels in the body are low. The production of ion lactate and other metabolites can cause a burning sensation in the muscles sometimes referred to as 'lactic burn'.
Loss of motor control	An *Hypoxic event* where the individual loses the ability to control movement in the limbs and neck. The uncoordinated twitching that takes place is also known as 'samba', and the victim may be fully conscious throughout.
Macro lens	A lens that magnifies images to reproduction ratios of 1:1 or higher.

Glossary

Manual exposure	Non-automated variation of camera controls that govern exposure, which includes *Shutter speed*, *F-stop* and *ISO*.
Marseillaise belt	Quick-release freediving weight belt made of rubber.
Megafauna	Large animals such as whales.
Micro Four Thirds	A camera system designed by Panasonic and Olympus of *Mirrorless interchangeable lens cameras* and camcorders.
Mirrorless interchangeable lens camera	A type of camera without a mirror reflex optical viewfinder, but which includes an *Interchangeable lens* mount.
Monofin	A fin used by competitive freedivers, which encapsulates both feet and has a single, large blade.
Myoglobin	A muscle protein found in almost all mammals, which bonds iron to oxygen in a similar manner to *Haemoglobin*.
No-fins constant weight	Competitive freediving discipline that involves descending vertically without any assistance from fin or line propulsion.
Partial pressure	Hypothetical pressure of a gas within a mixture, as if that gas alone was the only one present.
Peripheral vasoconstriction	Narrowing of the diameter of peripheral blood vessels (i.e. those not in the core of the body or that supply the skeletal muscles).
Port	Part(s) of a *Housing* which enable(s) accessories to be attached.
Prime lens	A photographic lens with a fixed focal length, as opposed to a *Zoom lens* with a variable focal length. Can also mean a primary lens in a combination lens system.
Pulmonary embolism	A blockage of the main artery of the lung or one of its branches. This can be from a gas bubble, which is more prevalent in diving accidents, or some other bodily substance.
Rear-curtain sync	Ability of some cameras to fire the flash just before the shutter closes. When combined with a slow *Shutter speed*, moving objects will show a low-contrast streak behind their direction of movement, to convey a sense of speed.
Sensor	Charge-coupled device also known as the digital photographic sensor, which is where an image is initially captured.

Shallow water blackout	Unconsciousness that occurs toward the end of a freedive, typically in the final ten metres of an ascent or at the surface.
Shutter speed	The time the shutter remains open. When less than one second, this is expressed in fractions of a second.
Snell's window	Underwater view of the surface through a cone of light. Beyond the area of the cone, the diver will see either darkness or a reflection of the underwater scenery.
SOUPA	Submersible Optics Underwater Platform Assembly. Modified float/ *Guide line* used to deploy camera equipment to a prescribed depth.
Split-level image	Image that divides the frame between an underwater scene and one above the water surface. Normally captured using a *Wide-angle lens* and dome *Port*. Also referred to as a 'split-world' image.
Static apnea	Competitive freediving discipline that involves floating face downward in water for a long duration (several minutes). Used as a way of proving elongated breath-hold. To avoid the risk of death from drowning after *Blackout*, this should never be attempted alone.
Strobe	Underwater flash unit.
Vasoconstriction	Narrowing of the diameter of blood vessels throughout the body as a result of contraction of the muscular wall of the vessels.
WDC, Whale and Dolphin Conservation	The leading global charity dedicated to the conservation and protection of whales and dolphins, UK-based. See whales.org
Wet lens	Conversion lens that can be attached and detached to/from a camera *Housing* whilst underwater. These typically provide macro and wide-angle capability. Also called add-on lenses.
White balance	An holistic adjustment of colour intensities so that neutral colours (greys and whites) are rendered correctly.
Wide-angle lens	A lens whose focal length is significantly smaller than the diagonal length of the digital sensor. Allows more of a scene to be included in an image and therefore a shorter subject to lens distance.
Zoom lens	A photographic lens with a focal length that can be varied, as opposed to a *Prime lens* with a fixed focal length.

Glossary

Index

Index

Index

Index

Index